A Thirty-Year Thought Journey

INDIA

SCIENCE, POLITICS, GEOSTRATEGY

GAUTAM R. DESIRAJU

गरुड

Published by
Garuda Prakashan Private Limited
Gurugram, Bharat

www.garudalife.in

First published in Bharat 2025

ISBN: 978-81-993915-7-4

Printed in Bharat

Modernists believe in a Lakshmana Rekha between science and philosophy. Prof. Gautam Desiraju argues against it in this book. Should scientists just mind their business? No! says Prof. Desiraju. Yes, scientists too should air their views on geopolitical-social issues. For that matter, it helps to examine such views, as the scientists have no conflict of interest. Prof. Desiraju demonstrates a need for the cultural and philosophical influence on science. He recommends that the large demographic dividend of Bhārat must be harnessed to create a larger pool of talent, aiming for global excellence. Intuitive driving may lead to more novel inventions, and we, the Sanatanis, may have an edge over others. As said in the national logo, Satyameva Jayate, we have always banked on seeking truth by questioning. We did not spare even the Lord; Arjuna frequently questioned him. And the Geeta is not another doctrine; the Lord gives freedom to Arjuna at the end, *yatha echchati thatha kuru*. This book is indeed thought-provoking.

—Dr. B. N. Gangadhar

Professor Emeritus, Department of Integrative Medicine; Former Director NIMHANS; National Distinguished Scientist Chair, Dept of AYUSH, GOI

While Prof. Desiraju's critiques on matters related to science and education over the last few decades have always been well acknowledged, his thoughts on political and geostrategic matters are equally compelling and insightful. Not only do his views make logical sense, but the real beauty is that they are delivered in a tone which is brutally forthright and uncompromising. Great to see the individual pieces compiled together in the form of this compendium!

—Rajiv Tayal

Former Advisor, Department of Science & Technology (DST); Secretary, Science & Engineering Research Board (SERB); Executive Director, Indo-US Science & Technology Forum (IUSSTF)

What happens when the rigorous logic of science is applied to the turbulent worlds of politics and geostrategy? This collection of essays tracks a 30-year intellectual journey, dissecting the foundational issues facing modern India. Moving from sharp critiques of Indian science and education to the heart of constitutional debates, the book culminates in bold geopolitical forecasting. It presents a compelling, data-driven case for the rise of 'Bhārat' as a civilisational state and the inevitable fragmentation of Pakistan. Provocative and analytical, this is an essential read for anyone seeking a unique and unflinching perspective on India's destiny.

—**Sampadananda Mishra**
Founding Director, Centre for Human Sciences, Rishihood University, Sonipat; Sanskrit scholar

"Silence is not an option for thinking people who are motivated by national self-interest." With this conviction, Gautam R. Desiraju brings together thirty years of reflections in *India: Science, Politics and Geostrategy*. Moving beyond the laboratory, he connects science with education, politics, and global affairs, showing how a disciplined scientific lens can uncover patterns others might miss. At once candid and thought-provoking, this book invites readers to engage with India's challenges and possibilities through the eyes of a scientist unafraid to speak his mind.

—**Swaroop Rawal**
Actor; Educationist

In *India: Science, Politics and Geostrategy*, eminent scientist Gautam R. Desiraju distils three decades of incisive commentary into an engaging narrative that connects laboratory logic with national and global realities. The compelling collection of essays takes readers on a fascinating ride through thirty years of observations, predictions, and bold ideas. From the state of Indian science to the shifting tides of global strategy, his sharp, clear-eyed reflections prove that curiosity and critical thinking can illuminate challenges far beyond the world of research. Written with scholarly rigor and intellectual courage, this volume offers a rare intersection of scientific reasoning and national discourse, inviting readers to examine critical issues through a lens grounded in evidence, clarity, and long-term vision.

—**Sunil Rai**
Educationist; Chancellor, University of Petroleum and Energy Studies (UPES), Dehradun; Served as a commissioned officer in the Indian Navy for 21 years, with postings on INS Vikrant, INS Nilgiri, INS Himgiri, and the oil tanker INS Shakti

To speak truth to power is rare enough; to re-examine that very 'truth' when needed is rarer still. In an era of polarised discourse, Gautam Desiraju brings such courage and clarity to questions that many avoid: from the crisis in Indian science and the shortcomings of the National Education Policy to the erosion of rigour in research, failing universities, and even the relevance of the Constitution and the Rajya Sabha. Anchored in data yet unafraid of provocation, his reflections compel readers to shake off apathy and reconsider their positions on issues as fundamental as education, governance, and the linguistic basis of India's states.

—**Sahana Singh**
Author; Commentator; Gurukula Champion

India: Science, Politics, Geostrategy could not have come at a more opportune moment when our country is at a pivotal point in its journey. Prof. Gautam Desiraju, through a selection of his articles in the last 30 years spanning a broad range of topics, offers us an intriguing mix of observations, deductions, and predictions in his inimitable style. I am glad that he decided to write this much-needed book.

—**Bhavesh Kansara**
Author and Satirist

Like an annotated diary of a scientist-seeker—personal, probing, and disarmingly honest. Professor Gautam R. Desiraju confronts, challenges and counsels Bharat. His conviction and clarity are on full display. A lifelong service to science and India, I laud his ability to connect disparate dots and compel us to rethink science, politics and nationhood with courage. Congratulations, Professor Saheb!

—**Arjun Kadian**
Author; Academic

In an age when our public discourse on important issues like India's future in a changing world has been reduced to social media ephemera and nightly news panel screaming matches, the essays in this book offer presence, insight, wisdom and guidance to anyone fortunate enough to want to take it. Gautam Desiraju's writings on science, education, geopolitics, and the peculiar cultural quirks of postcolonial India that make us chase delusions of global grandeur like awards and medals while losing the real treasures and strengths we have inherited over millennia make for a timely and rewarding read. If you are an educator, a policy-maker, a social media user, a student, or a parent, get this book, and read it frequently.

—**Vamsee Juluri**
Professor of Media Studies, University of San Francisco; Author of *Rearming Hinduism: Nature, Hinduphobia and the Return of Indian Intelligence*

This book is an excellent collection of writings by Prof. Desiraju on diverse topics pertaining to science, policy, and the general ecosystem. The author, endowed with pedigree, degree and scholarship, does a fine job of communicating his thoughts with eloquence and candidness. A reading of these essays leads one to discern his deep patriotism and faith in the innate strength of Bhārat. His overarching belief that Bhārat can leapfrog into a higher orbit of growth and claim its rightful place in the firmament of civilisational states comes out clearly in this book, which will surely motivate fellow Bhāratiyas in their vision of a Viksit Bhārat.

—**Vivekshankar Natarajan**
Professor of Marketing, Lamar University, Texas, USA; Bhāratiya

India: Science, Politics, Geostrategy offers thought-provoking perspectives on challenges and progress in Bhārat's re-emergence as a civilizational state. This curated potpourri of articles by world-renowned chemist and polymath Prof. Gautam Desiraju is accompanied by a commentary highlighting contemporary relevance on systemic problems in Indian science education in the context of India's socio-political ethos and geopolitical standing. No punches are held back in stating the problems, intrepidly countering misinformation, critically assessing the roles of multiple factors at play, and proposing sustainable home-grown solutions (e.g., rewrite the Constitution, reorganize India into 75 states). The remarkable clarity of thought and rationale are supported by eclectic bases e.g., in history, literature, science, statecraft, and Indic civilizational values. The deep erudition, out-of-the-box thinking, and delectable wit are hard to miss, making the book unputdownable.

—**Ganpati Ramanath**
John Tod Horton Professor of Materials Science & Engineering, Rensselaer Polytechnic Institute, NY, USA; WISE Guest Professor, Wallenberg Initiative Materials Science for Sustainability, Uppsala University, Sweden; Adjunct Professor, Indian Knowledge Systems & Mental Health Applications (IKSMHA) IIT Mandi, India.

One of the reasons science in India has struggled is that the younger generation has rarely had access to the vantage points once created and leveraged by pioneering scientists to make sense of the world. In this book, Professor Desiraju offers precisely such a vantage point—an invitation for young minds to glimpse what it truly takes to work at the frontiers of human knowledge. He reminds us that science requires not just method, but also mental agility and the courage to live deliberately in a world that is, and has always been, probabilistic. As he notes, "It is better to be slightly wrong at the right time than to be fully right when it is too late. This is true in science, in politics, and in geostrategic calculations."

With rare candour, Desiraju steps beyond the safety of academic convention to confront the messy, often combative arenas of science and public discourse. In doing so, he reveals not only the intellectual rigor of a scientist of the highest order, but also the vision of a public intellectual awakening India's civilizational spirit to help humanity break free from avoidable cycles of crisis. This book is both a treasure trove of insight and a call to courage for those ready to imagine science—and society—anew.

—Sanjeev Kumar

Dean, School of Liberal Arts, Bennett University, Noida

ॐ अचिन्त्यरूपायै नमः

Om Achintya Rūpāyai Namah

Salutations to Her Who Transcends All Thought

—**Sri Lalitā Sahasranāma** |554|

For the Srivatsa Gang

The moving finger writes; and, having writ, moves on:
nor all your piety nor wit shall lure it back to cancel
half a line, nor all your tears wash out a word of it.

—Omar Khayyam

Contents

Foreword

Some books inform. Some provoke. A few ignite. *India: Science, Politics, Geostrategy – A Thirty-Year Thought Journey* belongs to the last category. This work by Dr. Gautam Desiraju is not merely a collection of essays; it is the chronicle of a restless and fearless mind searching for patterns in the tumult of our times.

I have known Dr. Desiraju not only as one of India's foremost chemists but also as a thinker, who has dared to speak beyond the boundaries of his discipline. His pioneering work in crystal engineering brought him global recognition, yet what I have admired equally is his willingness to step into the public square, to question established narratives.

There are some issues, where both of us have agreed to disagree, because the views from the windows through which we looked at issues were different—but that did not come in the way of our remaining a mutual admiration society.

Dr. Desiraju is an original, bold thinker, never content with easy answers, never afraid to challenge orthodoxy. Over three decades, he has written with the curiosity of a scientist, the passion of a patriot, and the courage of a public intellectual who believes that silence in the face of truth is the greatest betrayal.

The essays gathered here began as spontaneous reactions to events, scientific, political, and geopolitical that shaped India and the world around him. Yet when read together, they reveal something greater: a consistent attempt to connect the dots, to see beyond the obvious, and to anticipate futures that were hard to imagine.

What happens when the rigor of a scientist is applied beyond the laboratory? These pages provide the answer. Predictions, projections, sometimes provocations: each piece is an act of intellectual courage. From his early concerns about the inadequacies of Indian science and education, his reflections evolved into broader questions: Can excellence and equity coexist in our universities?

One knows that there is nothing like intellectual democracy but including the excluded is so important for Bhārat. I was a member of the Moily committee on implementation of the new reservation policy in higher educational institutions. I remember on the very first day, I suggested that we must think of balancing 'expansion, inclusion and excellence'. In fact that became the main theme and the title of the report. This challenge still remains though.

Why has Indian science struggled to achieve great heights? What must Bhārat do to reclaim its rightful place in the emerging geostrategic order? Dr. Desiraju again and again passionately speaks about the importance of quality over quantity, which I share fully. In my article in Current Science titled "What will it take for Indian science, technology and innovation to make global impact?" I had said "They say that only those people are remembered in science, who say the first word or those who say the last word. How many times have we said the first or the last word? We have invariably looked through windows that others have opened up. When are we going to open up new windows ourselves through which others will start looking?"

Dr. Desiraju eloquently articulates the challenges that Indian Science faces in achieving the above objective, including why the Nobel prize has eluded us.

One of the most compelling aspects of this collection is its insistence that scientists cannot remain cloistered in their laboratories. They must bring their discipline of rationality, evidence, and foresight into the public arena. As a scientist myself, I resonate deeply with this conviction. The frontiers of science and the frontiers of national destiny are not separate—they are deeply intertwined.

Dr. Desiraju is unflinching when he addresses our colonial hangovers, our obsession with foreign recognition, and our hesitation to act decisively in global affairs. He reminds us that a rising Bhārat cannot afford timidity. In international relations, as he rightly notes, soft power follows hard power, not the other way around. These are hard truths, but necessary ones.

This book is both a record and a call to action. It calls upon all of us—scientists, teachers, policymakers, and citizens—to think boldly, to speak fearlessly, and to act decisively. Victor Hugo once wrote, "All the forces in the world are not so powerful as an idea whose time has come." Many of the hard hitting ideas in this book belong to that category.

Yet alongside his sharp critiques lies an undercurrent of hope—a belief that Bhārat stands at a critical inflection point. If we summon courage, vision, and discipline, we can shape not only our own destiny but also that of the world.

As I commend this book to you, I believe it will do more than inform. It will challenge you, sometimes disturb you, equally, some of you may disagree with what he says, but ultimately the book makes you think. And that, after all, is the true purpose of thought leadership—to push us beyond our comfort zones into the realm of possibility.

May this book spark the conversations that India needs, and may it embolden each of us to think one day earlier, to speak one word braver, and to act one step faster—for the sake of Bhārat and for the sake of humanity.

—R. A. Mashelkar

Former Director General, Council of Scientific and Industrial Research

Preface

This is a book that was almost not written. I was working on two major book manuscripts in 2024 and 2025. The first was a survey of Indian S&T in the extended time period from 1835 to 2025 in the context of heroes, heartbreaks and hopes, representing respectively the past, present and future of Indian science. The second was a scientific autobiography commissioned by the German Chemical Society in their series 'Lives in Chemistry'. While writing these books I was also thinking about various short pieces and articles that I had written about science and education in India, over the past 30 years, and which, in an indirect way, have served as a background for these longer books.

Interestingly, and since science in India has been related to socio-economic factors, my short pieces started acquiring a political slant after 2015 or so and there was a transition in my writing into political and finally geopolitical areas. Unlike pieces written by social scientists and defence analysts, my articles tried to view these matters through the lens of a scientist, in other words they begin with a hypothesis and go on to formulate a rationalisation or explanation for seemingly unconnected events—connect different dots in a way.

These pieces trace my thoughts on various matters of specific and general interest and, in this sense, form a basis for certain sections of the two major books mentioned above. A chance conversation with

Disha Anamika of Garuda Prakashan in June 2025 led to a discussion as to whether or not a book that recounted my thought journey from science to politics and further into geostrategy, through a selection of roughly 40 or so of these short pieces (out of the 120 or so that I actually wrote) with suitable annotations, might be of general interest to the lay reader, *independent of the two major science-related books referred to above.*

The present book is the outcome of these informal discussions and I thank Garuda Prakashan for joining me in this experiment with a 'different' kind of book. I also thank my enthusiastic coauthors, M. Bharadwaj, D. Bhattacharya, R. Mantri, R. R. Mishra, M. K. Mishra, S. Setty, M. K. Surappa and D. Vashisht who contributed to the writing of some of the selected articles.

—Gautam R. Desiraju
Bengaluru, 21 August 2025

Prologue

This book is a selection of essays, commentaries and articles that I have written in various magazines, journals and periodicals over the last 30 years as reactions to events that were going on around me and had struck me, in some way or another, during my professional journey as a teacher-researcher in chemistry in the University of Hyderabad (1979-2009) and in the Indian Institute of Science (2009-2025). In many cases, I had made predictions about what these events might lead to. These short pieces, and also my annotations on them during the writing of this book, convey my thinking over 30 years and hopefully show that any academic may naturally shift to a broader public platform, if he is adventurous and believes that the role of a teacher is to educate people in *any* subject of topical interest. I have tended to include more pieces from the last five years, and these largely concern political and geostrategic matters, notably pertaining to our constitution, to Pakistan, and to immediate political issues that face Bhārat.

This book is hardly an autobiography. The short pieces are merely a reflection of my thoughts at a given point in time; they always start with known facts and then attempt to extrapolate into the immediate or medium term future. I suppose one could call my scribblings and jottings reasonable projections. Since one is predicting things, one can always be wrong and like J. M. Keynes, I am always prepared to be corrected when the facts change. My annotations, I believe, convey this well enough. Nobody can be right all the time, especially in prognostication and yet I believe that I have generally been on the right track—this has also been told to me on more than one occasion by friends and well wishers. They say I seem to get to things long before others and this might explain why I have notched up a few successes in my professional life as a researcher in the chemical sciences. It was Leo Szilard who said that "if you want to succeed in the world, you don't have to be much cleverer than other people. You just have to be one day earlier." I view joining the dots as an intellectual exercise, solving a puzzle or code breaking, and as in science, feel that when a certain critical amount of correct data is available, it is possible to make reasonably accurate predictions about the future, whatever be the subject matter. In my case, my later articles have been concerned with our constitution, the nature of a civilisational state, the decline of the nation-state concept, the remaking of India as Bhārat, and a broad variety of geopolitical and geostrategic issues where the perspective of a scientist might bring to bear certain concerns that might have escaped others.

Scientists are rational and logical people, not given to extremes of emotion and reluctant to use words like 'always' and 'never'. We are more comfortable with words like 'generally', 'normally' and 'usually'. The maximum we will go to is 'unexpectedly' and 'surprisingly' and we smile when a colleague overuses words like 'novel' and 'remarkable'. We belong to a conservative profession. Because of the nature of our calling we just might be better at predicting events and happenings when compared to those in other professions, and specifically in predicting things accurately with a lesser amount of initial input data. We tend to be introverted, however, and normally do not share our opinions, especially with non-scientists and lay persons.

I may be different, however, from other scientists in the matter of sharing my opinions on topics of general interest. Living in India almost all my life, and having become settled in my job as a professor by the early 1990s, I started becoming aware of the inadequacies of our educational system, especially the way it had tried to handle the matter of advanced scientific research, although it has recognised easily enough by then that science was important for the technological and economic growth of the country. More importantly, and unlike the vast majority of my colleagues in the higher academic institutions of the country, I was unabashedly vocal about what I felt were serious inadequacies in our system. By 1995, I started writing about my concerns in a periodical called *Current Science*.

The 1990s were a period of great political confusion in India and the dominant role of the Congress Party gradually gave way to a coalition era where the Congress was obliged to support or include mildly leftist and caste or family based regional parties. This was the era of Mandal and the consequence of the 27% reservations for OBC candidates, both in educational and employment opportunities, had a big effect on universities and research institutions and the question was whether excellence and equity could ever go together. Gradually my writings began to acquire political colour. The problems associated with science in India seemed not to be entirely attributable to the scientists themselves but rather they seemed to be a consequence of broader political issues that had gripped a poor country that was trying to better itself and reconcile the seemingly irreconcilable. A number of pieces in *Nature India* and finally a review in *Economic and Political Weekly* in 2007 marked a distinct transition in my thought journey. An opinion piece in *Nature* in 2012 strengthened, to my mind, my 2007 views and held that the issue of science in India was indeed complex. Neither would more money necessarily yield better results nor indeed was the available funding India sub-critical at that point in time. The problems with Indian science must have been lying elsewhere, and remained buried in our history and in events long since forgotten.

At the same time, the increasing realisation among large sections of the people, and especially in the middle class, that our various attempts at nation building in what might broadly be called the Congress or Nehruvian dispensation, had not yielded fruits commensurate with the input effort, led to a situation where an alternative 'Idea of India' started gaining in acceptance. The coming to power at the centre of the Bharatiya Janata Party in 2014 heralded the coming of a completely different paradigm: a seemingly artificial idea called 'India' was seeking to remake itself as a much older idea called 'Bhārat', which had withstood the vicissitudes of time and tribulations, started reasserting itself. My short pieces, penned after 2104, reflected this new feeling of enthusiasm—that change might finally have arrived in our country, but they were tempered with a concern that the change was not happening fast enough. These mixed feelings applied not just to R&D and the educational sector but also to general political and geopolitical matters where I felt we needed to quickly re-calibrate our relationships with other countries: the world was changing fast. Science, in particular, was, to my mind, not seen as an active component of Indian political and economic decisions, and I started writing about semiconductors, pharmaceuticals and rare earth elements in the context of foreign policy.

Using the methods of scientific analysis, I next began to write about even broader issues, namely those concerning the nature of our country itself. What is a civilisation? What is a civilisational state? Are we one? If so, does our constitution reflect our aspirations and inherent nature and character? A book entitled "Bhārat: India 2.0" appeared in 2022 and another one called "Delimitation and States Reorganization: For a Better Democracy in Bhārat" came out in 2025. I wrote a number of supporting articles where I argued that the redrawing of interstate boundaries within Bhārat was a foolproof way of regaining our lost civilisational memory. Some of these articles find a place in this book.

Science is international and from the beginning of my academic journey 50 years ago, I have interacted with foreigners, especially those from the Western world. With dismay, I noted that the behavior of my colleagues in India towards foreigners, especially if they were white, revealed an obsequiousness and unnatural defensiveness that did not behove us as citizens of an independent country. It seemed to me that Macaulay had done his job well. Feelings of inferiority in general and with respect to white people in particular has been a hallmark of our society and it has crippled our economic and cultural growth as Bhāratiyas. This inferiority complex has also led to an unhealthy craving for awards in general, foreign awards in particular, and reaches a crescendo of obsession with the Nobel Prize that has eluded all Indian scientists since Raman's in 1928. A few articles in this book highlight these points.

Inability to handle foreigners, especially whites, were bound to have adverse effects on our foreign policies and I began to see connections with our missteps in this domain in former times with our colonial hangover. Today, after the change in government in 2014, and especially after Covid-19, we seem to be handling geopolitical affairs in a more mature and shrewd way, keeping our interests first, and worrying more about what they are rather than seeking the approval of the world outside of India. Some later articles are concerned with new geostrategic aspects of foreign policy that may be taken up only by a more confident Bhārat. Our recent well-considered counters to Donald Trump's outbursts and tantrums suggest this more mature handling of geopolitical matters.

The most refractory of our geopolitical issues is to do with our troublesome western neighbour, Pakistan, which is not a real country in the first place but rather a rentier state of the West. I strongly believe that Bhārat can only move forward if it settles the unresolved issues of partition both with Pakistan and Bangladesh and seeks to redraw maps in regions we may call, Bhārat, Bharatavarsha and Bharatakanda. A few articles on Pakistan and why I believe it cannot hold together as a sovereign nation for more than a couple of years, with or without US support, may also be found in this book. I wrote about a possible break up of Pakistan as far back as 2018. Today, many share my opinion and I feel good about this. Szilard was correct. It is important to be one day earlier than others. Let me modify his dictum a bit and say that it is better to be slightly wrong at the right time than to be fully right when it is too late. This is true in science, in politics and in geostrategic calculations.

Bhārat has reached a critical point in its evolution as a nation, at the present juncture. If it wishes to be taken seriously as a rising global power, silence in the face of actions by foreign powers in its immediate proximity, say as in the US bombing of Iran, or in its seemingly new-found interest in Pakistan, is not a good sign. We must wake up to the fact that in international relations, soft power follows hard power, not the other way around. Our aspirations to be a global leader will remain hollow unless we build a formidable military-industrial complex and develop the capacity to shape events beyond our borders. In order for this to happen, thinkers, teachers, scientists, academicians and thought leaders have to speak boldly without fear or favour. These elements of society are the ones who should lead the others whether they are politicians, bureaucrats, businessmen or common citizens. It is in the spirit of encouraging these sentiments that I have recounted my own thought journey over 30 years through these articles in open fora.

The Scribblings

Are scientists even responsible people, outside of their science? This is the question many might ask. Maybe lay persons think that we scientists are crazy folks in white lab coats with little practical sense and an inability to cope with the real world. If the reader has such doubts, then he or she should be reading this book. Scientists are ordinary people like everyone else. It's just that we do science instead of doing other things.

Should scientists try to communicate their thoughts and opinions on general and non-scientific matters to the general public? It is difficult for scientists to explain their research work to the general public because almost everything is lost in trying to simplify it for the benefit of lay persons. Science is a subject for specialists. It cannot be understood by non-scientists, as is any other professional activity. Where scientists *can* try and communicate with the public is with regard to matters where scientific methodology can be used to address general questions on economic, political or geostrategic issues. The reason I say this is that the experts in these fields are not accustomed to hearing views from hard core scientists about their issues. The thought processes of scientists are different from those of bureaucrats, economists, politicians, party ideologues or social scientists. It is well possible that a scientist's views on say, supply chains for rare earth elements, the break-up of Pakistan or why Bhārat is a civilizational state may prompt new thinking from subject experts in these areas.

People like me have been called amateurs in this line of activity—but very serious ones. Therefore I do think we have a place in the general socio-politico-economic discourse of this country.

Is it easier to communicate research findings in soft sciences like ecology, sociology and economics in contrast to hard sciences like physics, chemistry and biology? It is of course easier for a lay person to understand some very simple concepts in the soft sciences. Many of us would claim to say we understand something about climate change, body language or inflation as opposed to say hadrons, the Mannich reaction or epigenetics. So, while the soft sciences might appear to be more easily understandable than the hard sciences, I am sure that it is just as difficult for a practitioner to communicate the concepts and principles of these soft sciences to a general audience.

The following are complete extracts or selections from different pieces on the same or related topics over the past 30 years. In each case, I have made annotations or given explanations about why I wrote the piece. Sometimes I have gone back to the piece and tried to explain why I might not have been fully correct in what I said or wrote. Let me begin with the question as to whether we are polite or impolite in our discourses and academic exchanges.

This book presents a thirty-year stream of thought through a collection of my published articles, reproduced exactly as they originally appeared, without editing. The italicized text has been newly added to provide context, connecting commentary, explanations and extrapolations.

Polite and Impolite

Current Science, Vol. 82, No. 1, 10 January 2002

A. K. N. Reddy draws unnecessary distinctions between 'impolite' and 'polite dissent' (Curr. Sci., 2001, 81 735-736).

We Indians are unable to discriminate between professional and personal criticism. Hence our unease in being impolite. Professional criticism should be as harsh as possible. Otherwise the `natural selection', 'competition' and `diversity' alluded to by Reddy, will simply not emerge.

The politeness we witness could, in part, arise from fear. However, given the lawless and shameless climate generally prevalent today, I suspect a simpler reason for the politeness in Indian science — just plain and simple lack of confidence in one's own professional abilities.

The background to my short note is interesting. The editor of the journal, P. Balaram had written a piece titled "The Importance of Being Impolite" (Curr. Sci., 80, 1245, 2000) in itself a comment on J. B. S. Haldane's quip 50 years earlier that "science in India is developing with disappointing slowness because Indians are too polite." A. K. N. Reddy had tried to argue in favour of "polite dissent." My piece was a rebuttal to Reddy. Continuing this line of thinking, I feel that the problem with us Indians is that we tend to be polite when we should be impolite, as in professional matters, while we tend to be impolite when we should be polite, as in personal matters.

These issues do not seem to have gone away. I wrote an Op-Ed in THE HINDU (27 March 2025) very recently with M. K. Surappa on the poor quality of scientific publications in India. We were criticised vigorously by one of our colleagues in the IISc, not for the content of our piece, but for the fact that we were being rude and impolite to the Minister for S&T and the Principal Scientific Adviser to the Government of India. I reproduce the offending paragraphs:

The Minister's sense of delusionary self-comfort in having 5,351 Indian scientists figure in the list of the top 2% of scientists across the world in 2023 is downright bizarre. Rankings of India's 5,351 scientists range from 163 (highest) to 68,55,948 (lowest). In contrast, in Japan, 5,608 scientists figure in the top 2%, with their ranks ranging from 79 to 26,24,763.

Quantity is not quality. What is the quality of Indian publications when they are held up against harsh international benchmarks such as the Hirsch Index (H-Index) of our scientists and the Impact Factor (IF) of the journals where we publish? What is important is whether a paper is read widely, is useful to others, and, in the ultimate test, whether it is cited by one's peers. When judged by these benchmarks, the Minister's remarks smack of smug narcissism, nothing more.

Even as the scope and spread of the malaise in Indian science is justified through quantifiable metrics, a sense of false security has crept in, entrenched by self-deluding statements such as this one from one of the highest officials in Indian Science and Technology, the Principal Scientific Adviser, that "India is rapidly becoming a global research powerhouse". Such statements deliberately mislead and obfuscate.

> *I now leave it to the reader to decide whether polite dissent or open rudeness will win the day if the Augean stables of Indian science are to be cleaned. Anyway, who and where is the Hercules we are seeking?*
>
> *I now follow with two pieces which summarise much earlier thinking and which warn about the deplorable condition of science in India today. These are actually the second and third in a series that appeared in the Sunday Guardian in early 2023. These were written in the context of my having been inducted as a member of the S20 Engagement Group of the Government of India in late 2022.*

The Crisis of Indian Science

Sunday Guardian, 21 January 2023

Summary: The point of Indian civilization being accommodative of individual liberties and freedoms is worth reiterating, especially because science and religion in India have never been in conflict with each other. On the other hand, they have been in positive synergy.

Modern science, and by that we mean Western science, because it originated elsewhere, lacked the philosophical understanding inherent in our civilization. Undoubtedly, modern science has given us immense facilities and done a lot to reduce the hardship of daily life, but it has been disruptive and violent for our people at the social, mental and psychological level.

With all due respect to modern science and its handmaiden, the modern idea of "development" has been instrumental, in more than one sense, for all the major problems that we see around us today. These include war and terrorism, inequality, environmental crisis, natural resources depletion and most importantly, lack of faith among the educated classes.

We had also given a hint at the end of the first article, that not everything is hunky-dory in Indian science. Anyone who wishes to see better days for Indian science should be a trenchant critic of the way in which Indian science has been managed, done, and organised in this country.

There are three things that went fundamentally wrong with Indian science and its administration. First, when India gained independence from colonial rule in 1947, there was a dearth of resources. Grants or allocation towards science was not the priority for a newly independent nation. The fledgling nation had too many bigger problems to solve simultaneously. Historically speaking, the best science occurred in countries or kingdoms that allocated abundant resources for scientific pursuit. India, 2,000 years ago; America, about a century ago and Europe, about a few centuries ago. Wherever we go, the richest nations in the world did the best science.

A common counter argument to the above can be as simple as, "how and why did people like C.V. Raman get the Nobel Prize, that too when India was a colony and not at all wealthy?" This notion and line of questioning is not just fallacious, but also provides a peculiar sense of feeling good about our earlier achievements. Even the poorest countries have produced some brilliant minds, and will continue to do so. Such examples of excellence keep recurring sometimes, regardless of the social, economic, and political conditions that society around them may present.

They should not be taken as representative of anything.

Second, the biggest obstacle to scientific pursuit is the colonial mindset that we Indians continue to have today. After the two world wars, the United States dominated scientific pursuit. All vassal countries like the United Kingdom, Japan, Germany started to receive grants graciously from the Americans for similar pursuits. These nations continued to set the rules for the entire world. The American way of pursuing science had become the "legitimate" way of pursuing science. Today, however, this is being slowly challenged, with different poles of powers emerging across the world, making it truly multipolar.

However, just having enough resources does not in itself mean science is being pursued correctly. Such money intensive science is a brute force method, which focuses primarily on obtaining results quickly and can sometimes be an overkill. Today, the trend of pursuing postdoctoral study in Germany, Japan, the US, and the UK, in effect chasing the Western model, is common enough. Our social settings are quite different from the West. Hence, decolonisation is a must in Indian science.

Third, there was one man, more than anyone else, who was responsible for the death of Indian science. This was Saiyid Nurul Hasan, the education minister in Indira Gandhi's cabinet in the 1970s. Her pact with the Soviets in 1971 (by which the communists in India endorsed and supported, politically speaking) sounded the death knell for Indian science. The Indian education system started getting influenced by the Russian political outlook. Hasan was the executor of this grim agenda, which was systematically embedded into the system. A Marxist-Leninist approach to science was given a platform in India, because of the political environment of the 1970s.

Without excellent science, there cannot be technology. Many scientific milestones in India are, unfortunately, a result of borrowed scientific knowledge from other nations. It is not a result of our indigenous genius. While India notes the likes of highly paid expat CEOs like Sundar Pichai and Satya Nadella, we must be focused on producing homegrown vision leaders like Mark Zuckerberg and Elon Musk. A highly paid CEO is not reflective of any advancement in science and technology. What we need are startups based on DeepTech. An evangelisation on these lines is necessary.

Apart from all of this, the Indian bureaucracy is laidback and relaxed; political interference and the lack of any will to introduce deep-seated reforms have contributed to the overall scenario: Indian science is in a haphazard condition today. Globally, our universities are ranked far below the Western ones. The single author paper citations are average at best. The volume of papers published will simply not matter, if they are not well cited.

A combination of a colonial mindset, influenced by communism and disabled by an imperfectly implemented reservation system (whose true utility needs to be optimised) has limited the growth of scientific excellence in this great nation of ours. India needs to achieve the political will to overhaul the aforementioned. How do we go about it? This will be hopefully addressed in the third and the final part of this three-part series on Indian science in the G20 context.

> *Several serious problems like our colonised mentality, our obsession with Nobel Prizes, the ambiguous outcome of our reservation policies, the debilitating leftist influence on our education system and the fact that we do copycat science based on foreign models that might or might not work in India have been alluded to here. I have also advocated for trenchant criticism of the system if one feels strongly that all is not well. Silence is not an option for thinking people who are motivated by national self-interest. Let us be impolite.*

The Way Forward for Indian Science

Sunday Guardian, 27 January 2023

Summary: Science today must be executable by both poor and rich countries, with the promise of significant returns in the short run. This can only be effected by a country which is not on the sidelines, but is central—making India germane for this role.

The traditional Vannevar Bush research model is an orthodoxy replete with its own tenets of faith—papers, peer-reviews, patents and citations. This method is both inelegant and wasteful; a large pool of funds has to be made continuously available in a brute-force operation of relentless tinkering. The constraints of such a methodology are evident for a resource-strapped country with competing priorities—results are few and far between, with precious resources sacrificed at the altar of pursuing "top class" science.

Our second, and arguably more serious, concern with the Vannevar Bush model, is that translating scientific breakthroughs into practical life-changing technologies is a secondary process in the exercise. It is not automatic. Thus, it is moot to repeat the point made in our second article—the repeatedly toted statistic of India's third highest volume of papers in the world is meaningless, as our papers are almost wholly uncited. Innovations which hold utility for an average Indian's wellness and progress are thus stillborn or neglected while invaluable resources are pumped into a non-performing, self-serving system.

As a precursor to improvement in outcomes, we need a revolution in the methods which generate said outcomes. There must be more efficient and intervention-focused methods of doing science awaiting conceptualisation.

The kind of methodological sidestepping we hint at are central to leading Indian firms beating established western competitors. The legendary F.C. Kohli, the founding figure of TCS, solved a similar problem—how does one find a better, more efficient way of finding solutions in a procedural paradigm where copious money and idle time are a given for large players? He simply required his coding teams to get the code right within 10 tries, and 3 for getting the syntax right, in a world where competitors would stroll by with endless testing. Exceeding these limits would require you to explain yourself directly to Mr Kohli, an unenviable task. This method, and the attitude embedded within it, catapulted TCS to being a global force.

Indian science needs a similar relook into verticals which can touch the lives of the common man. We need better science for better living. India's own history points towards such approaches being a mantra for success. Take for example, telephony. The United States had almost complete saturation of wired phone connections by the 1950s. India continued to falter on this front well into the 1990s, with one absurd policy idea after another ensuring that waiting times for a landline connection would stretch into decades. Then came the unshackling of India's wireless telecom sector. The rest of the story is well known, with India leapfrogging into globally competitive wireless technology penetration. India it appears does exceedingly well in disruptive technologies being adapted, admixed and adopted. The beaten path of technological progression usually does not augur well for us.

India therefore needs to synthesize those disruptive technologies (verticals) that can have an outsized impact on citizens and business. A shameless importation of science done elsewhere, sufficiently modified to suit India's priorities, is a time-tested Indian recipe for success. It is true that this approach won't win us Nobel Prizes or get fanciful citation statistics, but it will provide the nation essential supply chain security, public welfare, and leading global businesses.

Five horizontals—energy, health, society and culture, automation, and food security—cry out for sustainable solutions, and verticals of disruption like AI, genomics, alternate energy, personalised health care, natural language processing, and quantum technology leading to a possible time reduction in Moore's law, hold the key to almost every conceivable technological solution which fits the rubric described above. In each of these five domains, India has some key advantages which can enable us to pivot towards a breakthrough-focused, exponential-technology-led model of scientific progress.

That said, it is pertinent to note the nature of breakthrough discoveries themselves. Pasteur's founding of stereochemistry or cure for rabies, Carrothers' discovery of nylon, Haber's fixation of nitrogen, or Bardeen and Shockley's invention of the transistor, were not born out of any vaunted national lab or within the serenity of academia. These breakthroughs were all outcomes of hard-nosed attempts at solving urgent industrial or societal problems, and the science caught up thereafter.

We have to understand a critical fact of the process—Vannevar Bush depends on the corpus of money and knowledge already generated within the system, and thus India is contending with a monstrous American and Chinese lead. The Chinese marshalled resources and time which we don't have, to reach a position where they will soon beat the Americans at their own game. It is untenable for India to run a race which it is destined to lose. Instead of choosing the terrain in a battle we are fated for defeat, it is far better to pick another battle. One only engages in a war with the idea of winning.

All is not lost—India has many preconditions necessary to take the rest of the world by surprise. There is a reason why ISRO can achieve what it does on a shoestring budget, and MNCs set up their bases in Bengaluru; India has numerous underlying strengths it can leverage, but sadly it has chosen a system of scientific research which hinders their utilisation. India's way forward is of disruptive innovation, exponential technologies, leapfrogging, moonshots, and private research into industrial solutions; The hobbling white elephant of concatenated government labs and overblown and overrated academic institutions has long outlived its utility. An "Indian" way of doing science is a sine qua non for achieving our longstanding ambitions, and to close the gap between us and our well-endowed competitors.

> *Two ideas are highlighted here. The first is that disruptive change may be needed in certain S&T sectors if we are to make any meaningful progress. This means abandoning our incrementalist approach to which we have become addicted. Both our love of incrementalism and our addiction to things like 'polite dissent' reveal fearfulness and feelings of inferiority which may have arisen because of a general lack of technical competence in our domain speciality areas. The second idea to come out in*

the above piece is that the Vannevar Bush model for R&D is not applicable to today's Bhārat. I have referred to this model again, in the context of the National Educational Policy 2020 (NEP), in a recent Op-Ed in THE HINDU (14 May 2025), written with Mirle Surappa. Here is a brief extract.

There is barely any evidence, four years on, that any of the NEP recommendations have been put into effect. In 2025, India's overall graduate employability rate is 42.6%, which is practically the same as the 44.3% of 2023. Similarly, knowledge-intensive employment in the year 2023 only stands at 11.72%. Multiple entries and exits, a hallmark of NEP, have only created low-quality and poorly paying e-commerce jobs.

The high rate of educated unemployment today shows that education in India is actually disempowering students. The NEP is a retreat to the Vannevar Bush model of the mid-20th century U.S. without its financial cushioning. The NEP is outdated and financially unviable in the India of 2025. With lip service paid to 'new' ideas such as Indian Knowledge Systems (IKS), mother tongue learning, changing history textbooks, flexible curricula and a complete absence of methodology to effect its recommendations, the NEP is a dead fish in the water. It depends on course choice alone to correct imbalances, notwithstanding that the course content itself may be unworkable. It is noteworthy that there was not a single member from industry or the business sectors in the committee that drafted the NEP.

I was recently introduced in a conference as the first noted academic to have taken a strong line against the NEP. It is not that the NEP is wrong. It is just that it plays safe and lists all sorts of desirable things that could exist only in a Utopia, not the rough-and-tumble India of today. It says nothing about how we should go about achieving all these nice things it advocates. As Sun Tzu says, "Strategy without tactics is the slowest way of winning a war". For a start, to bring about many of the changes recommended by NEP, the central government needs to use some of its political capital.

We move now from S&T to problems concerning education in general, where after 60 years of floundering around trying to get that elusive mix of quantity (equity) and quality (excellence), we have found neither.

Neither Quality nor Quantity

Nature India, 1 May 2008

Here, I track the loopholes in how India identifies and nurtures merit. This piece was written after the full onslaught of Mandal began to be felt in educational institutions. I kept warning people that if sub-standard people were admitted into PhD programs, one could not avoid them becoming sub-standard professors 20 years down the line. This has actually happened now in 2025. If you read this you will see that I was never scared of criticising a Union minister if I felt that he or she was saying something unreasonable or silly.

Twenty-five years ago, the scientific research scenario in India was simple. Life itself was simple. The number of institutions that undertook competitive research was small—the IITs, the IISc, some CSIR laboratories and a few universities. A small number of serious minded students undertook research. After a PhD, they would proceed for a post-doctoral stint abroad. Their parents did not ask them what their salary would be when they finished their PhDs. An even smaller handful, who returned to India, constituted a new generation of teachers. Life went on.

The research output of the country under this dispensation was by no means of the highest international level. A few scientists did aspire for this standard, and were successful in part. These scientists, however, were more the exception. They did what they did, not because of the system but despite it. Indian science was competent given its flimsy infrastructural support and near absence of equipment. It was a low input, low output, low throughput and low impact situation. Notably though, no one was anxious and making money was quite far from everyone's mind. A dedicated teacher and a few motivated students could together achieve a happy academic environment. Quality was the goal, and though elusive, there was never any doubt about identifying it when it came calling.

Change is knocking today on the doors of academia. Vast numbers of students aspire for educational opportunities at higher levels. In the name of democratisation, we have been told by our political masters to increase the outreach of our research programmes. Can the system cope with this increase? Over the last fifteen years, there has been a modest increase in the numbers of researchers who are able to publish their work in competitive international journals. This increase is, however, far outstripped by the numbers of research students, their general lack of quality, and their hunger for quick monetary gains.

Having evolved in more gentle times, the system is incapable of handling these enormous numbers. Our system is also incapable of handling populist political themes that promise to deliver education at all levels to the masses. It is equally incapable of handling ministerial statements that 12% of scientists in the U.S. including 36% of those in NASA are Indians thereby proving that there is nothing wrong with research in India (a statement made by D. Purandeshwari in the Rajya Sabha on 10 March, 2008). This minister also said that it was wrong to run down the country's higher education system since most Indians who excelled abroad were products of Indian institutions.

This is ludicrous. Is the minister implying that the Government of India is responsible for the excellent state of American science? Such statements make good copy in the newspapers but are far removed from reality. It is like saying that our space programme is a success because Sunita Williams has an Indian parent.

Research is elitist. It is impossible and unnecessary to make every student a high profile researcher. Research is elitist, exclusive, discriminatory, and at the highest levels of outstanding quality. Excellence in research is like high altitude climbing or marathon running. It is not meant for all. At more modest levels, a few more can participate, but that's the bottom line. Still, there is nothing wrong in moving from the slow paced quality based system which we had 25 years ago, to a more accelerated quantity based system, provided the ultimate goal is the identification and encouragement of true quality.

Quantity does not mean loss of quality. Quantity is also no substitute for quality. How does research fit into a quantity based system where everyone wants to study? Education must evolve in two stages: in the first stage a very large number of students must be given a sound undergraduate training in science, including laboratory work. In the second stage, a smaller number of truly gifted individuals must be identified and given a world class education. Simultaneously, those who terminate their education at the undergraduate level (and many should be encouraged to do so) should be provided with decent employment opportunities.

If identification and encouragement of quality is the true aim of a quantity based system, two indispensable elements are required for its successful prosecution: (1) The numbers of students processed at the lower levels must be really large; (2) The thoroughness with which the system is able to identify and elevate quality must be highly efficient. Both points require elaboration.

The talent pool is small. A key assumption in the working of a quantity based system is that the proportion of really talented individuals is always small and constant. So, in a heavily populated country the total number of extremely talented individuals is rather large. But the problem is one of identification of these individuals. It is like searching for the proverbial needle in the haystack.

Why does one need to educate a very large number of students at the undergraduate level? The main reason is that one cannot afford to lose the few individuals who are truly exceptional even as they remain hidden (even uneducated) amongst the vast numbers of more average people. Why should the screening mechanisms at the second stage of post-graduate education be very efficient? This is because we would be handling huge numbers at the undergraduate level. Unless our screening mechanisms are very efficient, the whole system would collapse under the weight of its mediocrity. With large numbers screened effectively, one would get the golden mean of quantity at the lower levels and quality at the higher levels.

What is happening today is sadly different. We have neither quality nor quantity. Our undergraduate programmes are in shambles. The students who drift into science only do so because they are unable to get into professional courses (however shabby the latter may be for the most part). They lack motivation, skill and even the ability to learn. The indifferent programme of study at the B.Sc. level converts most of them into zombies. This very group enters the post-graduate arena, once again because they have nothing better to do. We are forced to choose a smaller group from this jaded lot for our PhD programs as otherwise there would be no one to select. It is inconceivable that a system like this will deliver world class research outputs, and indeed it does not.

Can one think of a breakthrough in these dismal circumstances, as a way ahead? High levels of student participation at the undergraduate level demand budgets that are much higher than what we are able to conceive of in India. China has opted for this route and has set up 100 universities each with a budget of around 100 crore per year, and each handling 10,000 students. This would amount to an outlay of Rs 10,000 crore per year but nearly 2,50,000 students would receive a good undergraduate degree every year, and this is no small number.

I do not believe that a sum of Rs 10,000 crore per year for undergraduate education is large given today's realities (the DAE gets roughly Rs 7,000 crore every year) but there is a total lack of political will to take such a decision. The crippling administrative and bureaucratic set-up we have only compounds the problem. Sub-critical efforts like starting three IISERs, each admitting 65 students a year, and declaring that we will start two more IISERs, eight IITs, 15 central universities and 14 'world class' universities will take us nowhere.

Even if we are able to handle huge numbers of undergraduates, there remains the second question. Will we be able to identify the really talented ones from this pool and induct them into a world class programme of research? Our main problem is that we are simply unable to perceive quality any more. We have made so many compromises that we are now unable to even recognise that we are mired in a vast bog of mediocrity.

After 80 years of puffing herself up, India is unable to qualify to play hockey in the Olympics. But the rot had set in 20 years ago, and we were in a state of denial—unable to recognise it, or too scared to recognise it, or too corrupt to want to recognise it. In the end, the exact reason does not matter. Academics have kept silent for too long in a country that has stubbornly refused to identify and encourage quality. Disaster was inevitable and is now a reality.

In all successful countries, quality and quantity are two sides of the same coin of excellence. Because of this almost wilful neglect of quality India is paying a bitter price today in the field of education and research. Our main examination for the identification of research students, namely the CSIR-UGC NET, is in itself suspect. This exam tests students under high stress conditions, and encourages rote learning, and memory power. It does not test creativity, curiosity, non-linear thinking, and an ability to draw analogies, all of which are vital in research. We simply cannot afford to allow the students who qualify in this sub-standard test to enter our research institutions and expect world class work to emerge. It cannot and it will not.

> *Now in 2025 we have athletes like Neeraj Chopra winning an Olympic gold medal. But we still do not have Indian scientists winning big international prizes. Forget the Nobel Prize, which may forever be beyond India's reach. There are at least 10 top science prizes internationally and no Indian has yet been given one of these (Wolf, Kyoto, King Faisal). What are sportspeople doing right that scientists seem unwilling or unable to do?*

Liberating Our Universities

Nature India, 26 June 2009

It was only after my move to Bangalore and the Indian Institute of Science in 2009 after three decades at the University of Hyderabad that I was able to observe the University system more dispassionately, and for what it really is. It is rotten. I don't even know how I survived in the University system for so long. I prescribe here, mega doses of 'democracy' to bring life back into India's ailing universities.

It is no longer a matter of discussion that the Indian university system is discredited and disgraced. It is easy to dismiss our universities as bad. It is difficult to pinpoint the reasons. It is practically impossible to find solutions.

Universities abroad thrive for centuries on end. In India, they are barely able to hobble along after a few decades. In my early years as an academic, I used to wonder how universities in Oxford, Cambridge, Bologna and Cracow have lasted for a millennium, while once stellar universities such as Delhi, Allahabad, Mysore, Calcutta, Andhra and Banaras could not remain academically viable for even fifty years.

After thirty years in the University of Hyderabad, an institution I joined in its nascent days, I think I am beginning to understand how and why.

The leader holds the key. Unlike the Indian Institute of Science and the Indian Institutes of Technology, an Indian university is a personality-dependent organisation. Its prosperity and growth are closely linked to the competence, ethos and the morality of its chief executive. As long as this person is of impeccable character, the organisation prospers.

However, the administrative structuring of an Indian university is unable to withstand the ravages of an incompetent or dishonest leader. Each failed university in our country can be associated with just one bad vice-chancellor. The effects of such a person, it would seem, are irreversible and last long after he has demitted office.

The Government has rightly coupled its mission of higher education with the social and economic empowerment of classes that were traditionally excluded from these spheres. But the implementation of these agendas by corrupt and sub-standard people, who have little appreciation or concern for education in general, results in a deadly cocktail for disaster.

At this point, just about every young person who can, wants to rush abroad to get an education. He or she will take any chance, run any risk and face any consequence to avoid being educated in this country. The motto of my erstwhile university is 'education (is that which) liberates'. However, the real liberation, for our young people it seems, is to escape from the education on offer in our universities.

Appointing committees for vice-chancellors are typically made up of superannuated academics and administrators, many of whom have not even visited the university in question. The suggestions of this committee are then sent to the President of India or the Governor of the relevant state who makes the final choice.

This feudal and anachronistic procedure, in which there is plenty of room for political manipulation and chicanery, has no place in a modern, progressive society. In all successful universities of the world, the appointments of the executive authorities of the university are the sole responsibility of its own academic faculty—an internal matter, and accordingly a democratic and open matter. Only he who plays the game must make the rules. Committees of wise men in New Delhi often have little knowledge or appreciation for what is happening at the grass roots level in the education sector. They cannot be entrusted with this critical task of selecting vice-chancellors.

Working academics in the business of classroom teaching are the only ones who know the real problems of a society that is awakening both socially and economically. Good vice-chancellors need to know enough about academics to be able to identify talent. They need not necessarily be outstanding academics themselves. Good vice-chancellors also need to be savvy enough to attract private funding into their institutions, and not just live off Government subsidies.

None of these things are happening. Instead, a motley group of people with little comprehension of complex issues confronting them, head our universities. Their decisions are based on how it will affect their climb to the next step of the dizzying ladder that furthers them into administrative nothingness.

In such a scenario, the Government has been advised to scrap bodies like the University Grants Commission and the All-India Council of Technical Education, which have become autocratic oligarchies and laws unto themselves. In turn, it appears that a new super-body, a seven member Commission for Higher Education and Research (CHER), is being empowered to clean up the mess, with the Chairperson having powers similar to that of the Election Commissioner.

On paper this looks good, but in practice what guarantee do we have that the present rotten structure will not be replaced by another structure with seven Mughal emperors? The people who appoint the members of the CHER will, in all likelihood, be the same people who have been appointing our vice-chancellors, and the seven members will, in all likelihood, be chosen from amongst the present vice-chancellors. This is merely old wine in new bottles, not a route towards systemic change.

It is time to urgently embrace a bottom-up approach in which the stakeholders, that is the university academics, are the only ones taking important decisions. However, it is unrealistic and Utopian to expect that such a reality will emerge from the present system that is so heavily top-down in its approach.

There is a real opportunity here in the setting up of the new body CHER. The Government should charge CHER with the primary mission of democratising our universities and removing the shackles of bondage that have reduced them to skeletons. We are used to a top-down approach and know of no other method of administration. We need, therefore, wise leaders who are not scared to devolve their powers to the teachers. In my view, this would be the only way to liberate our universities.

> *Now, in 2025, I will say we have been lucky in that CHER was never set up. It would have been a case of old wine in new bottles. However, the government is now threatening to set up a body called Higher Education Commission of India which will replace the University Grants Commission. Shall we call this newer wine in even older bottles?*

In the above article, I wrote…

However, the administrative structuring of an Indian university is unable to withstand the ravages of an incompetent or dishonest leader. Each failed university in our country can be associated with just one bad vice-chancellor. The effects of such a person, it would seem, are irreversible and last long after he has demitted office.

I had seen a couple of bad vice chancellors in the University of Hyderabad, and the way their actions, or inactions, ruined the place. I decided to elaborate more on this theme.

Where are the Science Leaders?

Nature India, 7 May 2010

A critical deficiency in India's current scientific establishment is the dearth of credible administrators, who can rise to the challenges that confront her educational and research institutions today.

In former times, India's science establishment was led by 'stars', men of substantial scientific ability, entrusted with administrative responsibilities along with their scientific tasks. Some of these stars are still with us, perhaps not as luminous as before, generally bemoaning the lack of 'leadership' in the younger generation. One may well ask them—if this is actually true—who should be blamed for this lack of leadership today?

Indeed, one of the consequences of the star system is that the men whom these stars handpicked to succeed them to head our universities, national laboratories and research institutes, were typically people of only average to above average ability but who had the confidence of their mentors. These administrators bred similar successors and the inevitable dilution in this next phase of administration led to consequences that are now showing. The second lot of administrators owed their positions more to their patrons than to their intrinsic merits. So they were generally unwilling to take bold decisions to transform the scientific system.

What the stars and their successors failed to foresee was that the star system itself would fade out. This has happened in Hollywood, in

Bollywood, in cricket, in politics, and dare I say in organised crime and in public life, signifying an end to a mode of governance wherein a handful of heroic figures dominate the firmament.

In the context of scientific enterprise in India, the failure of the second set of administrators to initiate systemic change and the simultaneous demise of the star system has led to a dangerous situation—the appearance of 'professional leaders'. They constitute the third set of science administrators in the country.

Many of these newest 'leaders' are unusual; they are impelled to lead; it does not matter what they lead; it does not matter how well or how badly they lead. They just must lead. They would head a university, a fisheries board or a lottery agency with equal élan. They are single minded in their pursuit of the fishes and loaves of administrative office and they will do whatever it takes to acquire such office.

They have quite literally mounted the proverbial tiger that will devour them if they fall off. Simply put, they have nowhere to go if they do not hold an administrative position as they have long since abandoned science—the noble calling that got them anywhere near teaching or research in the first place.

In part, our method of selecting scientific administrators has got us into this mess. Screening committees are first created and these groups of wise old men suggest panels of names that other groups of wiser and older men scrutinise and in the end, the final choices are made after arcane procedures that involve the highest levels of bureaucracy and the political class. The ones who really have a vested interest in who gets appointed—professors and students of the universities, research personnel of national laboratories and scientists of the institutes—figure nowhere in the process. It's not very democratic if you ask me.

Because of this highly politicised procedure of appointing vice-chancellors and directors, many unusual outcomes ensue. Primary among them is that a leader, who has not grown within the organisation, is appointed. A rank outsider takes charge. Directors become 'professors' and professors become directors in a mad scramble for administrative authority. A vice-chancellor is appointed who has never taught a course, conducted an examination, caught a student cheating or defused a tense classroom situation with a joke; in other words someone who has not a clue as to what motivates or discourages students and faculty, gets appointed. Many directors today are unfamiliar with the research going on in their laboratories and have H-indices much lower than the scientists they administer.

It could be argued that a good administrator need not be a good researcher and vice versa. The argument begs the question, "What does one look for in a good science administrator?"

The following are three obvious and mandatory attributes: (1) The ability to hire good faculty or research staff; (2) The ability to attract public and private sector funding into the organisation; (3) The ability to convince employers in the market place that science graduates at all levels from B.Sc to Ph.D and beyond are employable and that an engineering degree is not the sine qua non for employment.

The situation looks grim. Those who are possibly the best qualified to lead do not seem to be willing to shoulder administrative responsibility, while the ones who seem to be the most willing are perhaps not as desirable. We need to be able to anoint true leaders who might lack the techniques to make themselves visible to the political class—by simply being too decent.

There needs to be much greater indignation and resistance to the present goings-on amongst the stakeholders in the system—students, employees, faculty, scientists—for, it is clear that the political class have little interest in identifying the reasons for the leadership crisis that now assails our educational and scientific institutions.

> *This was written 15 years ago and there was a certain delicacy in saying that many vice chancellors and directors sought their positions because they wanted to take money from the till. Today, there is no such reluctance to state that the majority of our academic 'leaders' are pilfering money left and right. In the state universities, vice chancellorships are literally for sale and the successful candidate is quite confident of recouping his investment in a relatively short period of time. When they are not corrupt, they are indescribably weak in decision making, for very often they follow instructions from the patron who secured their appointment for them in the first instance. Such is the condition of our educational system in India today.*
>
> *Among all our universities, however, Jawaharlal Nehru University (JNU) occupies a special place because it has been strongly identified with the leftist, Marxist, casteist cocktail of academics over the past 50 years and has come to be identified as the high temple of all doctrines that were criticised so stringently by the likes of Dharam Pal and Ram Swarup. The coming to power of the BJP was bound to affect JNU and the following article was written when it was still far from clear whether the BJP would be able to break the back of the leftist cabal that had once seized policy making in this country. JNU was also the bastion of many elements that were against the Babri Masjid demolition and the subsequent construction of the Ram Janambhoomi Temple. This is a longish article but one that I feel is worth (re)reading.*

Jawaharlal Nehru University: At a Dangerous Inflection Point

Swarajya, 1 January 2018

Summary: The essence of any higher level university is that it is a forum for constructive and progressive engagement between thoughtful, kind and enlightened teachers and questioning, critical and respectful students. The JNU has taken an altogether different path – in several unnecessary tangents.

Jawaharlal Nehru University (JNU) was established back in 1969. Even in 1965, when the bill for its formation was introduced in Parliament, it was held that this should not be just another university but instead a centre for "scientific socialism".

The first vice chancellors and senior professors at the university were all eminent educationists and administrators, but their leftist leanings were unmistakable. Over the decades, JNU remained a government think tank, notably for the social sciences, and as long as the prevailing political paradigm in the country was left-of-centre, as seen through the prism of the Congress idea of pluralism, and as peppered with a mild dose of Marxist thinking, all went seemingly well in this institution, with successive generations of professors mentoring students in their image and these students going on to become future professors.

Significantly, quite a few successful politicians at different points of the spectrum also began their political life in the student unions of

JNU, and this has played no small part in the aspirations of politically inclined students of the university till this day. The students, many of whom came from middle-class and lower-middle-class backgrounds, were influenced by the mild optimism generated by the soft leftist doctrines that prevailed during those years.

The essence of any higher level university is that it is a forum for constructive and progressive engagement between thoughtful, kind and enlightened teachers and questioning, critical and respectful students. Once this equilibrium is established, a university can go on for centuries, independent of the political realities of the day and which political icon is the flavour of the season.

The University of Bologna is nearly 1000 years old. It is still the best university in Italy. But Italy as a unified country has existed for only around 150 years. The University of Cracow is 650 years old. Poland did not even exist as a country for around 120 of these years, between 1795 and 1918. Wonderful universities do not derive their authority from the people in power in government. Much of the JNU's apparent strength arose from the fact that it was favoured by the benign gaze and patronage of the government in power in New Delhi. In general, such a situation does not provide for long-term stability.

The JNU issued a circular on 22 December mandating compulsory attendance for all regular registered students in all its teaching and research programmes. Without going into technical niceties as to whether or not this decision was ratified by the Academic Council or the modalities as to how attendance will be monitored in the various teaching and research programmes in widely disparate subjects, it is startling that any university, let alone a high-profile one like the JNU, can issue a circular of this sort. It is no mean feat to have provoked a protest both from the left-wing Jawaharlal Nehru University Students'

Union (JNUSU) and the right-wing Akhil Bharatiya Vidyarthi Parishad (ABVP), not to mention the Jawaharlal Nehru University Teachers Association (JNUTA). This is a warning sign, make no mistake about it. No self-respecting university will issue a circular mandating attendance because the whole educational enterprise is an essentially voluntary one. It is voluntary both on the part of the teachers and on the part of the students. Teachers are paid to teach, and they must teach because of that, but what they teach, how they teach and sometimes when they teach is, within curricular limits, variable.

As for the students, while they pay the fees, they come and go in the full knowledge that if they do not attend classes or laboratories regularly, they may not fare so well in their examinations/research work. A research student, who does not do their work regularly, in any subject, is not going to get a degree in a reasonable time frame. A miniscule minority at either extreme can be safely ignored. There are habitual malingerers who will not attend classes, and then there are brilliant students who get bored with the lectures and therefore choose not to attend. But we are talking here about the vast majority in between and the situation I have outlined above pertains to this vast majority. A good teacher-student equation is actually what prevails in any self-respecting university, including many central universities in India, which are largely able to maintain decorum and organisation, despite their many other serious problems.

I view the circular of the JNU administration therefore as a cry of despair. Teachers seem to have lost the trust of their students and students likewise of their teachers. Imagine a situation where teachers constitute a kangaroo court against the vice chancellor! Imagine a situation where students prevent a teacher from entering his office or where a 40-year-old is still considered a student! Of course, once you get on the tiger, you can't get off it and now both teachers and students are manipulated by a vocal and disruptive group who cannot bear to see an erosion of their falsely earned privileges.

The administration appears to be helpless. Clearly, classes as we know them are not being conducted at the JNU with any regularity, and neither teachers nor students seem to be behaving with any responsibility. Mandating attendance is not a solution to the huge problems faced by this university.

This latest 22 December circular cannot be enforced. Attendance records can be manipulated, and there is absolutely no guarantee that students will learn once they are physically in the classroom or the laboratory. No, the problems in the JNU run far deeper – this university has become a place where, because of the entitlements conferred on it by the powers that be over the last say, two decades, teachers are no longer teachers, students are no longer students and the university is no longer a university.

In hindsight, it is unfortunate that the Congress government of the day saw fit to create a university in order to have a think tank. Every government of a big country needs a think tank, and indeed our country is so big that it probably needs several of them to accommodate different viewpoints, but this could have been done in a more sophisticated manner, as for example the way in which the United States of America (US) has done with the Brookings Institution and the Trilateral Commission. When universities are chosen as think tanks in advanced countries, it is done with more subtlety and finesse than in our JNU experiment. The economic viewpoints from the University of Chicago are distinct from those that emanate from the Massachusetts Institute of Technology, and the US becomes stronger with this kind of pluralism. The JNU is now reduced to a shouting brigade that opposes everything that the government does—with no well thought-out, articulate reasoning. Words like "azadi" and phrases like "reclaiming the republic" have no meaning in a country where a solid 40-50 per cent of the voting population (that is, BJP voters) feel that they are quite free and are masters of their republic.

By making an entire university a leftist think tank and a laboratory in which dubious social science experiments are conducted, the government has let down the vast majority of teachers and students of the JNU who wish to just do their job properly. An honest teacher wishes to do his or her best by the students and in a research organisation like the JNU, they would like to carry out serious research that attracts attention and approval of the national and international peer group. An honest student would like to take advantage of the environment afforded by a prestigious central university like the JNU to broaden his or her outlook, and to use the education received there to obtain gainful employment after he or she leaves the university. Both these communities have been betrayed by the JNU management, successive vice chancellors and the governments over the past 20 years.

Undoubtedly, the problems of the JNU have become starkly visible today because (a) it has chosen to make itself an all-important touchstone of social and political discourse in the country, at the expense of serious academic activity; (b) there are now at least three alternative definitions for the "idea of India". Let me take up these points.

A university ought never to link its fates to one particular political viewpoint in the country. Political and social realities change, and sometimes rather quickly. The role of the academic community is to stay above these more mundane realities and aloof from them.

Sometimes the left is an agent of change, sometimes it is the right. The Gandhi idea of India is distinct from the Golwalkar idea and both these viewpoints are still distinct from the Ambedkar idea. Today, the voting population of the country is, roughly speaking, divided into three equal segments, each of which feels that just one of these viewpoints is the fastest, easiest or most practical route to economic well-being and national security. Elections are won and lost on these shifting perceptions. It's that simple.

The problem with some elements (the noisy, disruptive minority) in the JNU is that they believe that only the first of these viewpoints is the valid one. Even here, I believe that their understanding of the Gandhi-Nehru idea of India is flawed. Neither Gandhi nor Nehru would ever have countenanced a "tukde tukde" break-up of India, and yet the person from the JNU who espoused these views was courted and pampered by quite a few of our leftist intelligentsia and politicians in candlelight vigils and other such fake demonstrations (not in my India, etc).

Even more dangerous is that there seems to be prima facie indication that elements from the JNU are consorting with separatist forces in Jammu and Kashmir, and even worse, from Pakistan. The JNU is living in a time warp. It does not seem to realise that our issue with Indian Muslims today is not connected at all with Pakistan. It is our internal problem where we need to bring an economically and educationally backward group into the national mainstream. The latter has to do with a hostile foreign country, which we need to deal with using strategic geopolitical weapons—hard or soft. The radical Islamic influence, catalysed by Jammu and Kashmir separatists within the JNU is extremely dangerous not just for the university but for the country at large. The JNU is playing with fire, and our leftist politicians seem to have put their short-term interests above the country itself.

The preamble of our Constitution asks for "Fraternity, assuring the dignity of the individual and unity of the Nation". It does not speak about "tukde tukde".

Where the JNU community is now losing the confidence of the academic community and the general population is their perceived intolerance to viewpoints other than their own. In part, this may have risen from the inability of the Congress to accept that they lost an election in 2014—and that too so comprehensively. We live in a parliamentary democracy. We are never tired of invoking the sophistication of the Indian voter. It is quite difficult for one political party to secure a majority in the Lok Sabha. Let's concede this to the Bharatiya Janata Party (BJP). If the present government does not do its job, as seen by the voter, they will be duly voted out of office in 2019. India does not need the JNU to tell us that the BJP government is not good for the country, and certainly not every single day of our lives. We will be quite able to come to this conclusion in 2019, or otherwise, on our own. In the meantime, I think a great many honest tax-paying citizens are asking themselves as to exactly why they are subsidising this large, unproductive and now, frankly speaking, disruptive rabble called the JNU.

It appears that the teachers of JNU were having such a comfortable time doing practically nothing that they have now erupted at the first sign that their cosy status quo has been threatened. As for the students, they seem to have forgotten that their first responsibility is to their academic pursuits—and no, holding placards in Connaught Place and asking for the break-up of our republic are not recognised as academic pursuits, not by any stretch of the imagination.

To conclude, I will only invoke Zola and say "J'accuse". Or more provocatively, should I say that we may now safely remove the "U" from "JNU", so that it more appropriately becomes just "JN"? Take your pick!

Another summary: The problems in the JNU run far deeper—this university has become a place where, because of the entitlements conferred on it by the powers that be over the last say, two decades, teachers are no longer teachers, students are no longer students and the university is no longer a university.

Makarand Paranjape, a JNU faculty of long standing, has written a book about his university in 2022. It contains some ideas that I have alluded to four years prior to his book. JNU has now gone through with two BJP appointed Vice Chancellors and it is without doubt that the first of these, Mamidala Jagadese Kumar, has carried out some long overdue reforms in the university. The pendulum should always be swung to an extreme position in an ideological conflict, and make no mistake about it, this is an ideological conflict between a university and the Indian State. It is too early to tell if the second Vice Chancellor has made any systemic changes in the way in which JNU is run. A few battles might have been won but the war is certainly not over.

I have also referred to Pakistan, one of the first times I had done so in my short pieces. This trend continues till the present time as I view this so-called country to be an excrescence that must be excised. I will come back to Pakistan later in this book.

I now come to the matter of the Indian Institutes of Technology (IIT), a name that every educated and semi-educated Indian knows about simply because it is so difficult to get admission there. One has to run the gauntlet of an impossibly difficult exam the IIT JEE to do so. In 2024, 14,15,115 wrote the JEE

Main (first exam) of which 1,80,200 candidates qualified to write JEE Advanced (second exam) out of which 48,248 qualified for admission out of which 17,695 were actually given admission after the so-called 'counseling' procedure. The success rate is therefore something like 1.25%. I am always fascinated by these IITs. Who are these supermen who are able to get admission against such odds? Possibly this (perverse) interest in these institutions arose because I myself secured the 9th rank in the IIT JEE in 1969 and declined the same as I felt I had a better opportunity with a Chemistry BSc admission in St. Xavier's College, Bombay, a decision I have never ever regretted.

Quo Vadis IIT: Where Is It All Headed?

Swarajya, 24 June 2023

Poser: What would happen if the Computer Science B.Tech. program in IIT Bombay were suspended for one year?

With the annual proclamation of the IIT JEE Advanced results, the well-established custom of toppers' photographs being splayed all over our newspapers has followed suit.

We continue our ritualistic national worship of gods known and unknown, telling ourselves that yet again we have identified one more batch of geniuses who will count amongst the likes of Copernicus, Galileo, Newton and Einstein, and to those inclined towards more Bhāratiya heroes, Rishi Kanāda, Madhava, Bhaskara and Ramanujan.

These adolescents, we maintain, will reach pinnacles of glory, which will propel India to new technological heights. This yearly ritual worship of the new IIT entrants continues, even as only some of them will be able to resist the temptations of those precious green cards and dollar salaries, and stay back to restore India to her 'rightful' intellectual prowess.

The IITs, more than any other group of educational institutions, have come to epitomise the arena where we indulge ourselves in these flights of fantasy and phantasmagoria.

The feel-good factor drilled into us, and plastered all over our media, is inescapable. Even as we sit wretchedly in our individual pools of drudgery that characterise life in India today, while we worry about what an increasingly precarious future holds for our children, we see a set of seemingly incredibly focused youngsters who have subjected themselves to privations of the worst sort for many years, sacrificing an innocent childhood to surmount impossible odds and secure admission to the hallowed B.Tech. course in one of these IITs.

Indeed, the be-all and end-all for many young minds in India is to simply go through the hoops of the JEE by any means possible. Never mind that the interest of these youngsters in joining an IIT falls sharply after the seats in the five first IITs are completely filled. We like all of this. It makes us feel good. It's a curious mix of catharsis and delusion, where the permanent sequestering of young minds to memorise question-paper specific mathematical tricks is celebrated as a nationally essential conquest.

We feel that with JEE there is still hope for the middle and lower classes to jump to the upper middle class in a single generation. The thinking goes: what if you suffer to the point of physical and mental breakdown for five years if you can chill for the next fifty?

In an article I wrote 22 years ago in Current Science, I had stated, "All of coastal Andhra is dotted with residential outfits that train students to take the engineering and medical common entrance tests. Here the day begins at 4.00 a.m. and ends at 10.00 p.m. To my knowledge, the only other institution that worked successfully according to these hours was Auschwitz."

In keeping with the theme of Arbeit macht frei, the landscape is littered with suicides, mental depression cases, sleep deprivation, induced myopia, and considerable sociological and psychological trauma of students and parents.

For each IIT B.Tech. entrant, there are 100 unsuccessful candidates. What kinds of odds are these and what are the prevalent conditions which make so many parents subject their children to this hellish kind of Arbeit? What happens to the unsuccessful ones, and do the successful ones really witness a macht frei moment?

Above all, where are the toppers, the national heroes of yesteryears, after 30, 20, or even 10 years? How many of them reached that dizzying level of excellence that justified the annual polemics which come wedded with their JEE ranks?

I have had a ring-side seat in the Indian educational system for well nigh 45 years in two of the most well-known educational institutions in the country. I can assure you that one cannot entirely blame the parents for subjecting their children to the rigours of IIT JEE coaching, or their hapless wards who most often will listen to their parents unquestioningly. The absurdities of the IIT JEE, its corkscrew questions, the greedy coaching industry, and the hyper-anxious parents, whose behaviour sometimes borders on the tyrannical, are consequences of the complete failure of the education system of our country over 75 years.

The scandals surrounding predatory practices of coaching classes, which have erupted into the open in the last few years, are a damnation of the entire system. We fail our children, their parents, and the country year after year. And we still enjoy the spectacle. It is truly the Colosseum arena, not any old arena. Panem et circenses.

We have simply not invested enough in education. Any country that aspires for a higher quality of life for its citizens needs to put at least 2 per cent of its GDP to education and research, especially STEM research. Many countries invest more, even up to 4 and 5 per cent. In India it is a miserable 0.8 per cent, a number that has remained stagnant over decades.

Our education ministers, barring one, have been incompetent, to mediocre, to corrupt right from 1947 till today, no matter which political party is in power. I will make no exception.

Our state universities, which should be providing at least reliable job-oriented undergraduate education for everyone, are a complete disaster, wracked by caste politics, so-called self respect movements, reservations, political interference, corruption, and are run by politician-led education mafias and conglomerates.

In such a scenario is it that difficult to believe that all students will rush towards central government institutions no matter how hard it is to get admission?

As for the IITs themselves, the first 20 or so years were smooth, and they produced solid engineering graduates who acquitted themselves honourably. This observation stands despite many of them being forced to emigrate because of a total lack of opportunities in India. It was after 1990 that the trouble began. With liberalisation came a demand for software professionals and companies like Infosys, Wipro and TCS put such a high premium on an IIT B.Tech. degree that practically no one else could command a decent salary; even though these very companies spend millions of dollars every year to train and skill their IIT educated staff. The rush towards the USA became frenzied with the rise of Silicon Valley, and examples of IIT graduates becoming CEOs of top US companies only added to the frenzy.

Let us note that no IIT graduate has become a Bill Gates, Elon Musk or Mark Zuckerberg. They ended up at best as CEOs of giant American companies which is not the same as being innovators or geniuses. Essentially, people who were trained to be technologically nimble became glorified managers for American shareholders. In such a scenario one can judge for oneself the credibility of the Indian media, who project these IIT graduates as geniuses. These are merely 17-year-olds who have drowned themselves in the tricks of cracking the IIT JEE, and nothing more.

The prospects for Indian education are gloomy. We have had a history of repeatedly ignoring the excellent recommendations of education policy documents since the Radhakrishnan committee report of 1948 and the Kothari Commission report of 1964-66. If the past is any indication of future events, NEP 2020 will gently waft into the dustbin. The problems of language and caste have not gone away. They have become worse. We compulsorily need to conduct all our educational programs in our own languages, with English being an add-on wherever required. This is not happening.

Secondly, unless the elephant in the room, namely caste-based reservations, is done away with in its entirety, only despair and despondency among upper caste students will continue, leading to large scale emigration to strange countries. There is simply no room for meritorious students in India today. Is this not shameful?

In the meantime, the IITs will continue to flounder on. They have ironically become prisoners of their own much-vaunted B.Tech. programs. No research is done by B.Tech. students. So all this social media hype about the 17 year old topper wowing the world with his or her research acumen is just that—hype. In any event, all scientific research done in India is modest to above average at best. Even the avant-garde of Indian technological research is conducted under so-called "Global Capacity Centers" or GCCs, where cheap Indian talent does backroom work for multinationals, with India owning none of the intellectual property being produced.

The research in the IITs in basic sciences is honestly done but it is carried out by M.Sc. and Ph.D. scholars along with post-doctorals, not by the Ubermenschen who have cracked IIT JEE. IIT basic science research is, in any event, mostly not at the cutting edge of international competition. A handful of talented individuals in India who have attained international stature in STEM research are outliers. They are not even remotely representative of Indian STEM subject researchers.

The only ones who are benefiting today from this disgraceful situation are the coaching classes, who have rapidly grown into conglomerates toying with the idea of IPOs from being shady outfits run in the back-alleys of our major cities.

I like asking uncomfortable questions, and one of my favourite questions which I have asked to many fellow academics, especially in the IITs, is "What would happen if the Computer Science B.Tech. program in IIT Bombay were suspended for one year?". The best answer I have received so far is, "There would be a revolution".

I have said a lot in this article and it was roundly trolled by detractors and praised by admirers. This is in the nature of the game. Apart from the IITs, I have also talked about the impotent NEP and harmful caste based reservations. The older article is the 2007 piece in Economic & Political Weekly, which is too long to reproduce in this book. In a more hopeful piece, I have written about why economics should be taught more seriously to STEM students especially in the IITs and the IISc.

Economics as an IIT option

ETGovernment, 5 October 2024

It is interesting to note that the five-year integrated MSc program in economics has outpaced traditional streams like civil and environmental engineering for incoming JEE qualified students in the prestigious IIT Bombay. There is indeed a case to be made for students with a strong foundation in STEM subjects to take up economics as a career option. Economics is not merely a route to a high paying job in an air-conditioned office in Mumbai, Bengaluru or San Francisco. The subject has moved fast and afar—it would be no exaggeration to say that it is the only social science that attempts to put a quantitative footing to distinctly qualitative phenomena. The students who qualify in the JEE exam have a strongly scientific bent of mind. An imaginative syllabus in the IIT system and qualified teachers would enable them to address socio-political issues at a quantitative level and take the subject from being opinion based to data based, a feature that is critically important in the new Bhārat that seeks to find its place in the global order.

Historically speaking, economics has morphed from the discipline it was during the times of J. M. Keynes, the last of the qualitative thinkers, to the more quantitative paradigm that it is today. The end of World War II brought with it a sea change in the subject as America established its economic dominance via Bretton Woods, the IMF and the United Nations. Many disciplines made this qualitative → quantitative transition during the postwar period because of the appearance of the digital computer, whose compact size was facilitated by the parallel appearance of the silicon chip. Economics joined physics, chemistry and biology as experts grappled with complex problems and found solutions through mathematical and theoretical models. Economics became quantitative. Today it is the only discipline that seeks to explain qualitative ideas like incentives, choices and social phenomena in a robust quantitative fashion. It may not always have hit bulls-eye because at its core is human behaviour which is extremely hard to model and quantify. Nonetheless, economics has set for itself a more ambitious target than the natural sciences.

As human thought progresses, the desire and ability to quantify what are essentially qualitative phenomena will only intensify. The world has moved from the simple through the complicated to the complex. Economics is a tricky subject and it can lull many intelligent non-economists into thinking that it is easy to understand and follow, being apparently simple, even trivial. This, however, is a simplistic notion! A very important part of the modern discipline is causality, i.e, rigorously establishing a robust cause-effect relationship between the dependent variables and the outcomes using all theoretical and empirical tools at one's disposal. While such connections need not always be perfect, we have to give economics credit that it is the only social science that has even attempted to bridge the seemingly unbridgeable—qualitative and quantitative; analog and digital; intuitive and intellectual; imagination and reason. It is to be noted that scientists do not have to worry about causal phenomena. This is owing to the fact that they deal primarily with the study and explanation of the laws of nature, which do not vary with the whims of mortals.

Economics as a discipline has always been intertwined with politics. It would not be wrong to paraphrase Clausewitz and say that all politics is ultimately economics disguised in other garments—an anonymous quote from antiquity has it that when buying and selling is controlled by legislation, the first ones to be bought are the legislators. In a raucous democratic setup such as ours, it is indeed remarkable that politics has charted its own course with economics either playing second fiddle or being conspicuous by its absence. Or is it just hidden from plain sight? The time has come when rigorous quantitative economics is mainstreamed into our academic programs and in general into our society. NEP 2020 recommends a 4-year undergraduate program with multiple exit options; this allows science background students to pursue economics more deeply if they choose to—within say, the IIT rubric. Students can now opt for minors or majors in economics. The policy promotes research-oriented education from the undergraduate level, encouraging students to engage in research in areas such as development economics, public policy, and financial economics.

Good educational training and rigour will yield good economists but not everyone so trained may become an economist and need not be one in fact. Of greater importance is the inculcation of "economic thinking", an important facet leading to better understanding of real world phenomena and everything that is within the limits of sensory perception (emanating from the gross body, *sthula sharira*). However, "economic thinking" can go further into uncharted territory by quantifying the real world impact of what is sometimes beyond sensory perception, that is, that which is within the purview of the subtle body (*sukshma sharira*) such as deeply embedded likes, dislikes, choices, beliefs, preferences and motivations. This can do great wonders as it links non-deterministic causes to (somewhat) deterministic outcomes, an art in itself. The economic method and rigour can help to understand much of the wealth of knowledge buried in ancient and classical Indian texts by allowing us to take a more measurable empirical approach instead of the current qualitative benchmark. For example, in the Indian cultural context, one may use the economic method to design a robust experiment to test if belief in rebirth and karma makes people (and by analogy, societies) more environmentally sustainable as well as attribute the channel through which these outcomes are manifested. A brute force scientific approach or a purely qualitative approach would not suffice for such a task. However, the economics discipline, which links these methods, is a perfect candidate for studying such questions and hopefully, obtaining cogent answers.

In modern India, we have tended to lean towards qualitative thinking in the social sciences with institutionalised quantitative thinking having had a somewhat slower start. While this might have worked in the initial decades of our post-colonial journey, the inability to develop a community of quantitative and empirically robust economics researchers has led to the propagation of many half-truths, non-verifiable claims and non-robust assertions that have greatly harmed the societal discourse and at times even contributed to significantly lowering it. A well trained and dispassionate community of economics researchers in the country can do great service to correcting the discourse and prevent blatant propagation of falsehoods by snake oil salesmen whose first compromise is with the truth. The renowned science institutions in the country such as the IITs and IISc need to have a long-term strategy to make substantial investments in the propagation of economic thought. Others like TISS and GIPE perhaps need to take a more dispassionate view of things and possibly introduce some scientific content in their ambit. Training the next generation of economic thinkers will help us comprehend in depth the complexities of and interlinkages between modern multi-faceted politics, trade, societies, history, culture, financial systems and technology. Increased capital allocation by the government, affiliated educational institutions and the private sector are the need of the hour to create a wide body of economics academics and researchers that can help achieve this goal. That will indeed be the stepping stone towards a coherent and logical public discourse in a country as vast and diverse as ours.

And finally, it was the great Keynes who said that when the facts changed, he changed his mind.

> *While IITs are not specifically mentioned in the article that follows below, the implications are all too clear.*

For Make in India, Invent in India

Indian Express, 15 September 2023

Summary: The institutions that mediate the flow of capital and resources to convert scientific knowledge into technology-based wealth will require drastic changes to become effective and efficient so that these institutions power India's economic output

Bhārat is now the world's fifth largest economy and will make it to the third spot soon, but it lags behind on most benchmarks concerning innovation, science and technology. One of the main reasons for this deficit has been Indian academia and industry failing to ramp up its contribution to the national R&D effort. Manufacturing in key sectors has been hobbled by straitjackets in fundamental factor markets of land, labour and capital, as well as faulty trade policies.

Many of these errors have now been corrected, and while much remains to be done, the Make in India momentum is unmistakable with India's share of global merchandise exports registering fresh highs. Alongside the Make in India push, the government has recognised that the infrastructure to generate patents required an overhaul, and there is a strong effort underway to make it easier and faster to file for and obtain patents for inventions. Recent bilateral agreements in science and technology, especially with the United States, show that the government is correctly identifying strategic priorities in this vital sector, and appreciates that Invent in India has to complement Make in India.

But what will it take for Invent in India to build momentum and scale? The newly established Anusandhan National Research Foundation (ANRF) will hopefully address this important issue. The institutions that mediate the flow of capital and resources to convert scientific knowledge into technology-based wealth will require drastic changes to become effective and efficient so that these institutions power India's economic output to $10 trillion and beyond in the coming decade by delivering on productivity-multiplying R&D across industries.

The case for such reforms is self-evident — given its wealth of human capital, India has punched well below its weight in science and technology, and the status quo is out of sync with the country's broader economic aspirations, to put it mildly. As policymakers undertake the arduous but essential task of revamping key scientific institutions, we propose three critical parameters around which to design this overhaul.

First, merit and quality of human capital should be weighted the highest when it comes to staffing and administration of institutions. The bureaucratic mind or administrator's psyche is geared towards aggregating numbers, but in scientific research, Lotka's law reigns supreme, and losing the top dozen leaders in a given field to other countries is as good as ceding leadership of that field. The strong power law effect dictates that it matters far less that dozens of others might also be working in the same discipline.

Quantity is no substitute for quality. This reality of scientific research demands that India gears up to both retain its premier talent at home, as well as position itself as a home for talent from abroad. The remittance-seeking mindset of the Licence Raj era needs to give way to a value creation approach.

One of the principal flaws of science policy has been the near-complete separation of teaching and research. The footprint of research labs and centres across the spectrum of scientific institutions is scattered across India — many government labs could enter into structured collaborations with universities and where appropriate, synergise with on-campus science parks that could then expand their activities into industry itself. The idea should be to bring teaching and research together in a merit-driven admissions system.

Second, India should have a barbell strategy for funding research, with high convexity, high payoff projects getting their share of funding from a consortium of government agencies and industry.

There are two precedents for creating this barbell approach: The New Millennium India Technology Leadership Initiative (NMITLI) programme launched in 2003, and the more recent Design-Linked Incentive (DLI) programme. Where NMITLI made collaboration across industry, academia and national labs a standard practice, DU envisages underwriting innovation with big payoffs in collaboration with high technology businesses, with the India Semiconductor Mission receiving appropriate funding for semiconductor design. We suggest that NMITLI and DO are reliable models for setting the baseline on R&D, which should be oriented towards industry.

High risk endeavours, which have an outside chance for truly exponential payoffs, almost always originate from individual researchers. For such moon-shot research funding, a greater burden rests on the government even as innovative and entrepreneurial scientists should be encouraged to obtain supplemental funding from industry. Global business history shows how joint efforts by government and industry to fund blue sky research have yielded breakout results in areas such as pharmaceuticals, transportation, chemicals and telecommunications.

In several cases outside India where such results were achieved, the underpinning talent was trained in India but emigrated, which underscores the point on retaining our talent and prioritising merit in staffing and administration. Ultimately, bringing industry to the table for such outcomes should be done through the carrot of profit and the stick of competitive pressure.

Finally, alongside the institutional and hardware changes, the culture and software of Indian science too needs a reboot. It is easy to blame politicians for lack of progress, but they act on positions set by science bureaucrats who rely largely on domain experts in academia. Inevitably and unfortunately, this group becomes a self-perpetuating clique, with its own inertia and resistance to doing what is necessary, as that could upset a comfortable status quo.

While good system design for the new setup can incentivise collegiality, undermine hierarchical mindsets, eradicate cartelisation and promote controlled risk taking, eventually long term outperformance will be dependent on the quality and motivations of the people involved in Indian science. Possibly, we are not impolite enough, thereby reducing the quality of impartial peer review. A shakeup is warranted today, as the stakes are high not just for India's economic progress, but for national security too.

> *We discuss the lack of impoliteness in our discussions, the fact that teaching and research have been divorced in our country, and we say that there is a need to remake our institutions, for example the IITs. The IITs give a solid base and foundation but they need to be redirected in their mission and repurposed. Above all, admissions being made only through the IIT JEE is not a desirable situation. Students also need to be admitted based on legacy, economic strength and exceptional qualifications in domains that might not*

traditionally be associated with STEM subjects provided their academic qualifications are good. And finally, it should not be beyond the executive powers of the central government to ban coaching classes for IIT JEE altogether.

I will now recollect my thoughts about the attitude Indian scientists display towards foreigners, notably whites, and how this has led to a loss of imaginative creativity in them. The whole matter would have been amusing but for the fact that it is so sad that we have not exorcised the ghost of Macaulay from this country after nearly 200 years. We have a curiously ambivalent attitude towards white foreigners, alternating between xenophobia and slavishness. How much of this slavishness arises from the fact that $1 equals ₹85 and that any small coppers they fling at us is a large sum of money in India? Or that maybe even the xenophobia arises for the same reason?

The following article follows some discussion around 2004 that it was high time an Indian got a Nobel Prize in the hard sciences. A particular name was even being mentioned repeatedly. A. P. J. Kalam as President of India made a reference to the fact that an Indian scientist should be so honoured. None of these people even were aware of the fact that getting a Nobel Prize is an extraordinarily chancy matter and that a great many, often unknown and unimagined, factors are at play.

The Raman Effect

Nature India, 17 October 2008

Summary: India getting a Nobel is almost like buying a lottery ticket and silently wishing the odds are in your favour—as what is described by Munshi Premchand in his immortal kahani.

Another set of Nobel Prizes have been announced and one wonders why it has been so long since an Indian scientist working in India has been given this prize. Was C. V. Raman's prize in 1930 a fluke, are we simply not up to the mark, or are other factors at work? Is there any connection between the fact that we do not get Nobel Prizes and that we do not win many medals in the Olympics, or produce a Wimbledon champion, and that generally we do not fare well wherever individual excellence is assessed by the highest international standard?

Do we lack a killer instinct, an ability to exhibit the premeditated aggressiveness that presumably characterizes a winner? Or are we burdened by a system, a society and a mindset that simply makes the whole business of consistently winning big international prizes laughable?

More prosaically, it is instructive to view the Nobel Prize as a commodity and the winning of it as a commercial activity that leads up to its successful marketing. This activity has three sequential components: inputs, outputs and the technologies that transform inputs into outputs. The inputs in this case are the group of Indian scientists who might, under favourable circumstances, be able to win a Nobel Prize. The enabling technologies are the measures employed by our scientific establishment to ensure that outstanding Indian scientists become world leaders.

These measures should ideally be characterized by a system of rewards that clearly correlates with scientific output, by unimpeachable standards of accountability and by the overall honesty and transparency with which they are administered. The outputs in the Nobel Prize enterprise are the set of traditions, guidelines and rules that are employed in the selection of the prize winners and the manner in which Indian scientists might fare in such a system of evaluation.

This last 'outputs' component of the exercise is completely outside India's purview and influence, and so I will not discuss it further except to say that it operates at a very high level of rigour and honesty. In my own subject, chemistry, one can think of many deserving scientists who have not been awarded this prize, but one cannot think of even a single undeserving candidate who has been given the prize in recent decades. The message is clear: the Scandinavian academicians who select Nobel laureates have been doing an impeccable job and the winners are picked from among those whose work is not only novel, but has also fundamentally changed the ways in which we think about our respective subjects. Alternatively, the work is of a type that has had a far reaching impact on people's lives and livelihoods.

Clearly not all excellent work merits a Nobel Prize. An Indian, or anyone else for that matter, has to run a stern gauntlet before he or she is even remotely within the limits of consideration for this award. Nobel Prizes are serious things, and they cannot be discussed in a breezy way by the popular press, as has been done in our country.

There is some consensus that all is not well in India with the second 'technologies' stage of the Nobel Prize enterprise, in other words the way in which the scientific system identifies and nurtures talent within our country. What is required, if indeed the aim of the game is to secure Nobel Prizes for India, is a system that is able to discriminate objectively and then encourage substantially. Assuming that one has a number of competent scientists, the system must be able to identify the really outstanding ones using dispassionate criteria that are blind to all factors save academic excellence. The next step would be to encourage such scientists in all possible and perhaps even untested ways. We are uncomfortable with both these activities.

Over the last 60 years, we have become used to a socialistic pattern of thinking. Our society today caters best to its average members and is not able to cope with the outstanding. It is very easy to tailor a system to suit the needs of the average person—this requires the least amount of thinking. Coping with the outstanding person implies that one is able to firstly identify such a person, and this requires both work and honesty. Encouraging an outstanding scientist is also hard work—the system should not hesitate to operate outside its comfort zone, and this is truly difficult for the Indian science bureaucracy.

It is in the first 'inputs' stage, however, that we face our most serious problems. When it is commented that a country of our size is not winning Olympic medals and Nobel Prizes in relation to its population, it is forgotten that most of our population is not brought into the sporting or scientific/educational stream in the first instance. Effectively, we are a "small" country. We lack both the ability and the means to bring into the scientific pool, all those who are inherently capable of doing creative work. In most parts of our country, even access to primary schools is difficult.

Those who do manage to go to school have to cope with an arcane and byzantine system of education that compels rote learning and kills creativity. Assuming that some students make it through all this nonsense, our society places such a high premium on the irreconcilable elements of job security and monetary gain that our best students continue to opt for the engineering course, which appears to be the only one that provides some ephemeral satisfaction with respect to this oxymoron of high paying secure employment. Good scientists are risk takers who revel in the unknown. Therefore we are hardly likely to have a large pool of good scientists in a conformist society such as ours.

It is not a question of this or that particular Indian scientist winning a Nobel Prize. The USA secures so many Nobel Prizes because at any point in time, there are say 100 American scientists around, any one of whom may get a Nobel Prize depending on specific shifts in emphasis in the subject, changes in the economic, political and social climate of the world (yes, these are important even in the science prizes), personal preferences of the award jury members and a host of other factors, both objective and subjective. These filters are numerous and unpredictable. Only with a large input pool of contenders will a country stand a chance of consistently securing Nobel Prizes. It has taken Japan sixty or so long years of sustained all-round development before it has entered the Nobel Prize stakes in a big way. India today does not have even five potential Nobel Prize winners. Some say that we do not have even one. In such a scenario, what chance is there of an Indian scientist ever winning a Nobel Prize?

I will end, as I began, with C. V. Raman. Perhaps his prize was a fluke. Perhaps it was not. Raman was an outstanding intellectual and the Indian Association for the Cultivation of Science, the place where he did his prize winning work, was an example of an untested model for institution building, outside standard comfort zones. The system did not identify Raman, but he identified the IACS, and that was enough.

Nobel Prizes cannot be planned in advance. A chance discovery often starts off the process, but the astute scientist recognizes such a discovery and develops it into a major theme. Many recent Nobel Prizes in physics and chemistry have been awarded to people whose work made substantial inroads into academic and industrial activity far removed from the original work that was ultimately recognized. In such a scenario, Nobel Prizes are won by individuals not through premeditated activity but by virtue of the fact that they work in countries where there is overall high level progress in the educational and scientific spheres. A future science Nobel Prize from India is therefore quite unlikely. Even assuming for some reason that it comes to pass, it would be a matter of pure chance. And we all know that winning a lottery is the rarest of happenings.

Another summary: Over the last 60 years, we have become used to a socialistic pattern of thinking. Our society today caters best to its average members and is not able to cope with the outstanding. It is very easy to tailor a system to suit the needs of the average person—this requires the least amount of thinking.

We seem to be obsessed with Nobel Prizes probably because we all sense that no Indian is going to get one anytime in the near future. Of course one can argue and say that even Donald Trump wants a Nobel Prize, so who is anyone to say that Narendra Modi should or should not want a Nobel Prize?

In a humorous vein, let me say that the one good thing about Nobel Prizes is that they cannot be given to dead people! I could write another book just on this topic if this were not the case.

And a final hilarious one on Nobel Prizes! When you say ₹100 crore, you're talking serious money. And this is the amount Chandrababu Naidu mentioned.

"Rs. 100 Crore from the Govt If You Get the Nobel Prize" Is Not How You Get One

Swarajya, 8 January 2017

Summary: You would need at least 25 scientists at the top level in a country if any one of them is to have a sporting chance of getting a Nobel prize. Announcing cash awards is not how one creates the environment needed for innovation and excellence in science.

A Nobel Prize is the most serious and solemn distinction that can be bestowed upon a working scientist. It is always given to a scientist who is alive. In the 100 odd years of its existence, there might have been many cases of deserving scientists who did not get this prize, but one would be hard put to identify an undeserving scientist who got it. The venerable Swedish professors who constitute the Nobel committees certainly seem to know their job well and this award is one which stands above all others in the world of science.

So, when Chandrababu Naidu, the Chief Minister of Andhra Pradesh, declares that he will award Rs 100 crore to any scientist from his state who wins this prize, I can only conclude that he knows very little about science, even less about the Nobel Prize, and almost nothing about science in Andhra Pradesh.

Winning a Nobel Prize is like securing an Olympic gold medal or winning the Wimbledon title. There has to be a general scientific temper in the environment, there must be a ruthless system in place where only merit is rewarded, and where the members of the scientific community are only loyal to maintaining the highest possible quality in their subjects. For various historical and cultural reasons, India has a lot of catching up to do in all these respects. Rightly or wrongly, international science is carried out, evaluated and rewarded according to a value system that is based on a reductionist approach which began during the Renaissance. This model was perfected in Europe in the 19th and early 20th century. It then migrated to the US and finally to Japan. It is no wonder then that most science Nobel prizes go to scientists in one of these countries.

A critically large ecosystem to nurture a very high level of scientific activity at the topmost international levels simply does not exist in our country. The degree of brutal honesty and objectivity that is required to sustain very high level science also does not exist in India. Nobel prizes are not obtained by going for the latest fashionable areas of research in the West and trying to do more of it in India by purchasing fancy equipment at exorbitant prices. Nobel prizes are given for real breakthroughs, for introducing new ways of thinking, and for absolutely new and unexpected discoveries. There is very little correlation between the amount of money put into a research project and the likelihood of this work securing a Nobel Prize for the scientist involved.

There is too much hoopla surrounding Nobel prizes in India. Shipping in Nobel laureates to the country and parading them here and there in the name of making people aware of the importance of science is probably a waste of money. Perhaps, this makes for good press and provides immediate titillation to a few but it cannot result in any long term impact. Asking questions to Nobel laureates about how to go about getting a Nobel Prize is equally silly. All of them will tell you that they do not know how and they are correct because nobody enters the scientific theatre with an idea of securing a Nobel Prize. They say the only way you know for sure that you were nominated for the Prize is if you get it. Such are the levels of secrecy employed by the Swedish Academy of Sciences.

The sad part of Naidu's statement is that he was probably convinced that he was saying the right thing. This can only mean that he does not appreciate the real benefits that good science can deliver to his state or to the country. He seems to feel that if a scientist working in Andhra Pradesh were to magically get a Nobel Prize, this would be some sort of endorsement for himself and his policies. He also does not understand the dynamics with which quality science operates and the fact that you would need at least 25 scientists at a Nobel level in a country if any one of them is to have a sporting chance of getting one.

Finally, even at the local level, he does not know the inadequate state of scientific activity in Andhra Pradesh. Only yesterday, a colleague told me that of the 1,100 fellows of the Indian Academy of Sciences, not one works in Naidu's state post-bifurcation. Naidu has to do a lot of homework, and his advisers have to advise him a lot better before he makes these rash statements about science. Otherwise, he is in danger of becoming a laughing stock at least in competitive scientific circles.

India is a huge country with immense potential for excelling in science. Our large under-30 population is our biggest asset. The story of Indian science since 1947 has been a sad one because so much more could have been achieved with a talent pool that is this highly gifted and motivated. It seems sad to think that the likes of J. C. Bose, M. N. Saha, S. N. Bose and G. N. Ramachandran did all their glorious work in this country. With this kind of potential, it is the duty of responsible politicians to harness our talents and set up a system that is based on honesty, accountability and fair play in science. Only the politicians can do it because only they have the authority to do so.

Naidu would be better off if he were to address these serious and important issues rather than announce such cash awards. Considering what the Nobel Prize is, I can say with reasonable certainty that no Nobel laureate who is awarded a cash prize of 100 crore would accept it, whether he were from Andhra Pradesh or anywhere else in the world.

> *Serious scientists are not driven by money. If a Nobel Prize is shared by three scientists, which is often the case, each would get the equivalent of around ₹3 crore each. Where is ₹3 crore and where is the ₹100 crore Naidu was wantonly promising? Did he even know the implications of what he was saying? Worship of the West and Western institutions must stop forthwith if we are to have any future as a Viksit Bhārat 2047.*
>
> *I had begun to think more seriously about religion by the late 2000s, and by that I mean my own religion, that is Sanātana Dharma, a name I much prefer recently to Hinduism, which is a Western import. My religion is not an -ism whatever else it might or might not be. Indeed the difficulty in classifying Sanātana Dharma and neatly pigeonholing it into this or that silo is practically impossible but the codes and doctrines of the religion are incredibly well laid out—a typical complex system, to use scientific jargon. The reader will note that I have used the words 'Hinduism' and 'Hindu' way back in 2007. Today I would definitely prefer 'Sanātana Dharma' and 'Sanātani'.*

Finally, let no one let go of the fact that Sanātana Dharma is a religion and not a way of life. Those who call themselves spiritual but not religious are probably bluffing or are extremely hypocritical. I don't mind someone calling himself or herself atheist or agnostic but somehow this 'spiritual' word grates on me. Even here there are limits. In a recent meeting with a scientific colleague over several days, he would begin each day telling me he was an atheist. After two or three days of this, I told him that something must be troubling him about being an atheist if he was referring to the matter so often. For example, I don't go about running here and there telling people I am Sanātani. I have to do it here because I am writing a book on this subject!

In God We Trust

Nature India, 2008

Indian scientists and their religion are seemingly inseparable. The results of a recent survey conducted by the Centre for Inquiry in India and Trinity College, Connecticut, on the religious beliefs of Indian scientists, are hardly surprising. The findings state that the majority of us, mostly Hindu of course, believe in the existence of a higher power, while a quarter among the believers call Him God. The study also records the beliefs of Indian scientists in reincarnation and karma, their predilection for seeking Lord Venkateswara's blessing before an important scientific venture, their attitudes to the caste system and so forth.

Why am I not surprised? For a start, India is deeply religious in its inner ethos. The importance of spirituality to life has been reiterated by our seers and sages over time. To say that religion is a crutch used by poorer civilizations (since wealthy countries have dispensed with religion as superfluous) is to oversimplify and trivialize the matter. India, except during 1800-2000 AD, has never been particularly poor. The economies of India (and China) have always been important to the economy of the world, except during this interregnum. Again, small yet persistent numbers of people from supposedly richer climes have been continuously attracted to Hinduism, seeking a solace from it that eludes them in say, Christianity. Hinduism appears to answer and satisfy the metaphysical needs of affluent societies where the daily necessities of life are no longer an issue.

Further, Indians seem to be uniquely able to synthesize irreconcilable states of being, whether sublime or ridiculous. We tolerate total squalor amidst unimaginable riches, high thinking alongside venal corruption, female infanticide with abject mother worship, cricketers raking in crores in a six week IPL season while most of the country ekes out a living, garbage from clean houses making for filthy neighbourhoods, public impoliteness amidst great personal courtesy. Does it surprise one then that many Indian scientists say they are deeply religious?

It is tempting to attribute this ability to synthesize disparate and even contradictory themes to our religion, which has seamlessly amalgamated features of other religions as it has grown from strength to strength. But science is different in that it is sternly objective. There is this point of departure where science comes into conflict with all religions. Science is about induction from fact while religion is about deduction from dogma. A careless mix of religion with science can be disastrous. The West has experienced this catharsis several times over since Galileo′s encounters with the Inquisition. Hitler's theories of eugenics and Lysenko's on the inheritability of acquired characteristics illustrate the conflict between true science and other religions—Nazism and Communism—and the consequences were equally appalling. I think therefore, that the results of the Trinity College-CFI survey ought to be taken seriously. Does the survey indicate in some way that Indians are inherently incapable of doing really good science because of their religious failings?

The scientist follows a conventional and well accepted protocol. He formulates a hypothesis, designs experiments to prove or disprove it, and then analyses and rationalizes his results. The eventual goal is towards a theory which may ultimately lead to new laws. This inductive approach was refined further by Karl Popper′s ideas on falsification. Popper stated that no number of positive outcomes at the level of experimental testing could confirm a scientific theory, but that a single counter-example would reveal that the theory, from which the implication was derived, is false. Therefore disproving a hypothesis is more important than proving it and a theory that forbids is more powerful than one that merely predicts. Science makes no preconditions on the outcome of an experiment but it demands that cause and effect follow each other inexorably until the final truth is revealed. The big prizes in science go to those who dare to be different and do not fear being proved wrong. All this is quite far from organized religion as we know it.

There are, however, situations in modern science where an insightful combination of science with religion and philosophy may bear fruit. A persuasive instance arises in the study of complex systems and emergent properties, where the behaviour of higher level entities may not be predicted or anticipated in a straightforward way from the properties of lower level objects. In such situations, one cannot rule out the role of scientific intuition which goes beyond mere intellect. But such intuition is not illogical. Rather, it is super-logical. It is built on a bedrock of knowledge and organized thought. The importance of intuitive knowledge is stressed in our religion especially in its *advaitic* formulations and it could well be that Hinduism, at its highest levels, has something unique to offer to the solution of complex scientific problems.

As a chemist, I will quote two spectacular examples from my subject where intuition played a key role in a path breaking discovery. The first is the postulation of a cyclic structure for benzene by August Kekulé who dreamt, they say, in ouroboric fantasy, of a snake swallowing its tail. The second is more recent and about how Francis Crick and James Watson arrived at the double-helix structure for DNA. It is said that their eureka moment came when the crystallographer Jerry Donohue told them that they were using the wrong tautomeric structures for the bases that form the essential core of DNA. They realized at once that this was why they were unable to put together a sensible arrangement of hydrogen bonds in their original model of the superstructure, and the rest is history.

Science claims that it dispassionately tries to seek the truth. But do scientists (or anyone else) understand what is meant by truth? Is truth relative or absolute? Can science find truths only within the paradigms of Newton, Maxwell, Gibbs and Einstein? Are there other frameworks that we do not know of and are therefore beyond comprehension, competing realities that can co-exist with the one given to us by these scientific greats? These are esoteric questions, but closer to ground level, it could be said that a blind belief in religion might lure a scientist away from rigour and discipline, perhaps even without his knowledge. The dread of such laxity is perhaps why many Western practitioners of science shy away from religion to the extent of calling themselves agnostic if not outright atheistic.

At the very root of the matter, religion asks one to suspend rational thinking and substitute it with faith. We Indians are a religious bunch one way or another. While science is about questioning, religion is about acceptance and submission. It is easier to accept things than to question them. Is belief in religion then, a feature in societies that are lazier and more cowardly rather than in those that are poorer? It seems to me that it is this lazy streak in us that makes us accept religion so easily. But ironically, the same laziness will also lead us to think less seriously about religion. So it would appear then that Indian scientists are neither that religious nor that good at what they do.

> *The above article mentions truth. Is it absolute or relative? Keats said "Beauty is truth, truth beauty" and we all know axioms do not require any proof. Is quality truth? Do different people perceive quality differently? Do different people perceive beauty differently?*

In Search of Quality and Truth amid a Blizzard of Wokeness and Virtual Reality

Firstpost, 15 May 2024

Summary: Today, quality has become individualistic, as society becomes lonelier and has split into single voices over social media.

Quality and quantity are two sides of the same coin, each trait contrasting the other. In any aspirational society, the blind motivation is to capture and own both; a state of everything, everywhere, all at once! Without balance and modicum, it becomes one virtue at the expense of the other. Voltaire, ever pragmatic, stated that the perfect is the enemy of the good. In striving for excellence, one would not even achieve the good, as these two aims are an inherent contradiction. What is the best is often not the quickest resolution. Einstein was more idealistic, valuing quality over quantity; thereby pitting one directly against the other. In the end, the civilised world turns with a healthy tension between quality and quantity, striving for a synergistic convergence of the two traits.

Bhārat today has a huge demographic dividend, a quantitative advantage over our competitor China. In India, 26 per cent of the population is aged between 10 and 24, while 25 per cent of people are in the 0-14 age group, according to United Nations Population Fund, UNFPA. About 18 per cent of China's population is in the

10-24 age group and 17 per cent in the 0-14 age group. What are we doing with our population dividend? Not very much, I am afraid.

After I voted in the recent election in late April, I posted a simple selfie on X that showcased my voter's mark rather prominently and asked voters to just go out there and vote. The post had a mere eight words. Within 24 hours, it had 1.1K likes, an unreal number for me, given my modest engagement with X. I have never got so many likes for a post, including several I quite liked myself viz. well-considered opinions of current events, that barely made it past double digits. So I asked myself what it was about this innocuous post that "grabbed eyeballs".

Going back to Occam's Razor, a ploy I often rely on, I came to the conclusion that most people reading my posts in X or anyone else's for that matter, lack basic cognitive, analytical and logical skills. Mind you, X has a relatively small number of subscribers in India, perhaps two crore at the limit, and all of them presumably have some working knowledge of English, although their grammatical and spelling skills are nothing short of deplorable. X is important because its contributors tend to 'shape opinion' and the potentates within this group are anointed social media influencers. I have no idea what they might influence. Now, the inescapable conclusion is that most readers of my posts, nearly 20K of them, are too lazy to read or even try to understand what I have written. A photograph, that too a casual one of me voting and showing off my inked forefinger, does not tire or exhaust their brain. All of them are eligible voters, I assume. Each of them would have identified with my post because they saw themselves in it. And this is why they punch that like—the easiest thing to do on a holiday. This is what our demographic dividend is doing.

Cogito, ergo sum, I think therefore I am, said René Descartes. Our magical educational system has produced masses of people who cannot think—therefore they are not. Examples of this abound freely in the public space. A 28-year-old was elected to Parliament in 2019. There were 'psycho'phantic reactions that predicted a future Prime Minister. A 38-year-old, who just might make it into Parliament this time around is facing such a daunting fate today. As if it is that trivial to become Prime Minister of India! And then there's the Rajya Sabha, the inevitable dumping ground for all these shrill English TV debaters. Whither this august body?

Those students who make it through the monkey mills of the IIT JEE and UPSC exams, the so-called success stories of our system, know facts, in fact too many facts. Their brains are chock full of facts. But we forget that information is not knowledge, and knowledge is not wisdom—not by a long shot. What India needs are knowledgeable and wise people, not walking libraries. Anyway, why do we even need libraries? Everything we need is available with Google and ChatGPT. Before long, AI will dispense with human beings altogether.

To the so-called successes of the Indian education system, I would point out that Swami Vivekananda said that education is not the amount of information put into your brain to run riot there undigested all your life. He also said that the very essence of education is actually the concentration of the mind, not the collection of facts. We see a manifestation of things running riot in the posts on X and other social media platforms. We will have produced millions of mental hooligans and vagabonds, not responsible citizens, who should guide the less fortunate members of society forward responsibly.

What we need for Bhārat to achieve its rightful place in the world is quality. In trying to seek the golden mean between Voltaire and

Einstein, one must ask how quality may be identified. Quality is so difficult to define, that in the age of machines, it has simply been quantified. Anything is quality if one has oodles of it; houses, cars, foreign labels, even disciples on social media. Einstein actually expanded his observation and elaborated that not everything that can be counted counts and not everything that counts can be counted. How true this is and how far we have deviated from this essential truth. And yet, truth is given the go by in the age of post-truth. We inhabit a culture where emotions and personal beliefs often override objective fact and evidence in shaping public opinion. We saw an example recently—the DGP of Hyderabad closed the case on Rohith Vemula on the grounds that his caste certificate was a fake. There was an immediate outcry from students and political parties and it is now sought to reverse the findings of an investigation that had completed its work seven years ago.

What is truth? Unless this can be answered, we will not be able to identify quality. Quality has four essential attributes: (1) it must be a group decision; (2) it must be time independent; (3) it must be culture independent; (4) it must arise as a result of human activity. Let us look at these four conditions.

Today, quality has become individualistic, as society becomes lonelier and has split into single voices over social media. An individual cannot proclaim quality, only a critical mass can. Swathes of readers consider Shakespeare, Austen and Hemingway to be writers of the utmost quality. Equally, the Ramayana and the Mahabharata are revered as great literary works. Fitzwilliam Darcy and Karna, King of Anga, are etched in our minds for all time, as they embody universal qualities, both good and bad. When quality is identified by critical numbers across culture, country and conceit, the particular extends to the universal. Such evaluations stand the test of time. An adoring echo chamber of semi-educated people in a book release function in Lutyens' Delhi cannot make a quality evaluation that will stand the test of time. Once quality is reduced to individual vanity, it has no relevance. This is what we Indians fail to understand.

Quality must be time independent. The literary works mentioned above span centuries in human history. If one considers the Madurai Meenakshi temple, the Kinkaku-ji Temple in Kyoto, the Sacre Coeur sepulchre in Paris, the Empire State Building in New York City and the Burj Khalifa skyscraper in Dubai, one recognises a certain similarity in these man-made objects built across the centuries. All of them exemplify quality as they span the grounded earth to the limitless sky, propelling our imaginations to unimaginable fancies. True quality has a very long shelf life because it is time independent.

Quality is also culture independent, and nowhere can this be seen so clearly as in the fine arts. Who is to say that the cave paintings of Ajanta are superior to the Sistine Chapel ceiling or to Picasso's Guernica? Who is to say that Yehudi Menuhin or Vladimir Horowitz are better than Bismillah Khan or Lalgudi Jayaraman? No one can. All these people and phenomena represent quality at the highest level and are culture independent. They evoke strong feelings of individual joy and collective euphoria when viewed, heard or observed. In a fascinating musical comparison, the similarities between Beethoven's Moonlight Sonata and Muthuswami Dikshitar's kriti, Chandram Bhaja Manasa, both written at the turn of the early 19th century are striking. Clearly, the moon evokes similar emotions across widely different cultures, and in the skip of a heartbeat, the specific transcends to the universal.

Quality is created by humans and is enjoyed by humans. The appreciation of quality is an essential part of a full life. Therefore, it is an obligation of humans to be able to identify it correctly and preserve it properly. We Bhāratiyas find ourselves at a critical juncture in our intellectual and moral development. We need desperately to be able to identify true quality in a world that is being battered by political currents and counter-currents, by a blizzard of wokeness, virtual reality and an inability to distinguish the truth from what is not. Our national motto is Satyameva Jayate. This is all very well as long as we are able to define satya. This is the challenge that confronts all of us.

> *A major shift in my general, and by that I mean my non-scientific, literary output came around 2018 or so, just after my formal retirement when I started reading about the Indian constitution. I had been observing scientific and political happenings around me for 20 years by then and began wondering why things had to be so very complicated in India from the smallest of day to day incidents going all the way up to the safety and security of individuals and indeed the country itself. The Mumbai terrorist attack in 2008, the failure of the then government to take retaliatory action and the general lawlessness prevalent among the ruling classes and the ruled made me wonder why things had come to such a sorry pass.*
>
> *When I started reading the Indian constitution, a document that I didn't even know existed till then, I was in for a shock. I mean this was the document that is supposed to be a blueprint for governance in any civilised country and the first thing that struck me was that, unlike many constitutions in the world, there was no mention of the word 'God' anywhere in the document. In the end, the Indian constitution is the longest in the world and this omission struck me as bizarre, considering that Indians are a deeply religious lot, whatever be their denominational preference. I felt that even without mentioning this or that specific god, a*

reference to 'God' itself would have caused no harm or injury to anyone. Going forward, I began to realize that our constitution was largely a cut-and-paste effort from British customs and traditions, notably the Westminster first-past-the-post electoral procedure, American practices and sentiments, a garbled subjective view of federalism, Irish emphasis on rights and most disappointingly the fact that more than 60% of the document was directly lifted from the 1935 Government of India Act which is more a set of procedures that a colonial conqueror needed to keep his subject natives in check rather than a system that an independent country would want to choose for itself. I wrote around a dozen pieces based on my thinking over the last eight years or so and I reproduce here just a few of them, giving references to the others.

During this period, I completed my first non-scientific book "Bhārat: India 2.0", which emphasized that Bhārat was the correct name for my country and not India, that it was a civilizational state and not a nation state and that its citizens, Bhāratiyas that is, were those who subscribed to the cultural norms of Sanātana Dharma even if they were of varied religious denominations. Of particular importance are the 22 crore Muslims who inhabit Bhārat, and who constitute the second largest religious group in the country. I emphasised that the Muslims are not a minority in India but rather that they should be treated as the second largest majority. This was still a novel idea when my book came out in September 2022. Naturally I started thinking about Pakistan and the Muslims who went rather than those who stayed behind.

Let me now share some articles centred around the above themes. The first was written two months before "Bhārat: India 2.0" was released. It contains ideas pertaining to linguistic states and the desirability of a new constitution. Karnataka has been chosen as a case study because it illustrates many of the problems associated with linguistic states. I have also referred to the quasi-federal nature of the Indian State and also to the desirability of scrapping the Rajya Sabha. I will take up Karnataka again towards the end of this book. The ill effects of linguistic states have been more clearly enunciated in my second non-scientific book on "Delimitation and States Reorganization: For a Better Democracy in Bharat". A very recent article on whether or not Hindi can be a national identifier is also included.

It was around this time, I mean 2018, that I started wondering about why I was taking a different road with respect to my short articles, getting more into politics and non-scientific topics. I recapitulated Rumi who has said that "as you start to walk on the way, the way appears". This sounded more friendly to me than the well-known Frost quote on the path less chosen.

Let's move on…

India 75@75: Case for Smaller States Has Never Been as Convincing as Now

Swarajya, 11 Jul 2022

Summary: India is too big to have just 28-and-odd states plus smaller Union Territories. Is it too unreasonable to ask for 75 smaller states in the Union of India as a gift we give ourselves on this 75th anniversary of our independence?

India has 28 states and eight Union Territories today. In terms of population each state has on an average 49 million people. The equivalent numbers in the US with its 50 states, and Switzerland with its 26 cantons are 6.5 million and 330,192 people.

Clearly, our states are too big simply in terms of the voice that a citizen has in our representative democracy.

The origin of these states is a curious mix of our colonial history and subsequent developments wherein certain deeply felt needs to affirm local identities coupled with the Union's responses to strategic and administrative concerns came together.

The colonial legacy gave us a patchwork of areas directly administered by the British (British India), and other areas, the princely states, which though nominally ruled by their royals, had no real sovereignty of their own in any constitutional sense.

It was clear even in 1947 that the administrative distinctions between the provinces of British India and the princely states would have to go. Sardar Vallabhbhai Patel was the first to move in this direction and did away with the idea of respecting any paramountcy that the princes might have enjoyed in the days of the British Raj. The necessary empowerment was given to the Union through Article 3 of our Constitution, a provision that remains unchanged till today. It was also evident that some of the presidencies of the Raj were too large and diversified leading to a cumbersome and inefficient administrative set-up. Smaller states are always easier to administer.

The British had, in their time, separated Bihar, Orissa and Assam from Bengal, and Sindh from Bombay. The first major new state in independent India came about when the Andhra and Rayalaseema regions of Madras were separated in 1953 and further expanded through the States Reorganisation Act (1956) to include all Telugu speaking areas of the country in a new state Andhra Pradesh.

The concept of linguistic states was thus born and it proved to be a resilient template for many decades, especially in southern India and also in the division of Bombay into Maharashtra and Gujarat in 1960.

The division of Punjab into Punjab, Haryana and Himachal Pradesh in 1966 was born out of the demand to create a homeland for the Sikhs but even so, the unspoken strategic need to have a small state on our western border with a troublesome even inimical neighbour was simultaneously and silently satisfied.

The division of Assam into seven North East states followed natural impulses driven by cultural, ethnic and linguistic differences in this crucial region and was accomplished smoothly over a period of 40 years with some of these 'seven sisters' proceeding through a UT status before achieving full statehood.

The first move away from linguistic states occurred when Uttarakhand was hived off from Uttar Pradesh in 2000. Chhattisgarh and Jharkhand are similar although one notes that the demand for a separate Jharkhand is more than 100 years old, dating back to the colonial era.

Major realignment of state boundaries almost always followed from agitations that arose from deep-seated feelings of establishing what were felt to be genuine regional identities that had a true cultural, historical or societal basis. The case of Telangana is surely exemplary, also because the two portions of Andhra Pradesh that were created in 2014 are of comparable size (unlike Uttarakhand and Uttar Pradesh).

The state that was the first example of a linguistic state was also the first example of a non-Hindi speaking state to be divided into two, demonstrating perhaps that there are truer measures of identity than language that are relevant today.

Karnataka is an interesting example in point and one can consider it as a case study. The modern state had its beginnings in the princely state of Mysore, a dominion that was noteworthy for its highly progressive administration that emphasised social, economic, industrial and yet, also Dharmic upliftment of its people. Other Kannada-speaking areas from the Bombay and Madras presidencies of the erstwhile Raj as also from the princely state of Hyderabad were amalgamated in 1956. The state has been reasonably well administered over the years and is also politically stable. And yet Umesh Katti, a sitting minister in the present Bharatiya Janata Party (BJP) government, has said that Karnataka will be divided into two and India will have 50 new states after the next Lok Sabha elections. He further adds that "Prime Minister Narendra Modi himself will take the initiative on this issue". North Karnataka (or Hyderabad Karnataka), from where Katti hails, is indeed distinct from the southern part, the old Mysore state with its main grid in the Bengaluru-Mandya-Mysuru corridor, in the matter of history, geography, climate, culture, language and diet.

Karnataka is nominally Kannada-speaking but undoubtedly Hindi and Marathi have significant numbers of speakers in the northern parts.

Bengaluru is a virtual polyglot paradise and it is quite easy to live in some newer parts of the city without knowing a single word of Kannada. In any case, it is so close to the Andhra Pradesh and Tamil Nadu state borders that Telugu and Tamil are also well understood.

This brings us to another issue that has cropped up in many large states — one huge metropolitan area develops to the detriment of the rest of the state. In this connection, Katti rightly says that Bengaluru city is overcrowded, and lacks water supply for citizens who have to spend hours in traffic jams.

Katti also said, and in my view rightly so, that it was high time that IT companies thought beyond Bengaluru. The chief casualty in the lopsided development of Bengaluru has been Mysuru, a city of considerable charm and with a potential to become a centre for micro, small and medium enterprises (MSME) and light industry. It remains a neglected Cinderella.

Katti's concerns are mostly well founded and the division of Karnataka into smaller states would almost certainly bring economic development and improve the quality of life of the people.

While we are on this topic one also might consider that there have been long standing demands for separate states for Tulus and Kodavas, very distinct communities from old Mysore and also north Karnataka. So maybe Karnataka needs to be divided not into just two but perhaps three or four smaller, more easily administered states where the true identity of its people would be able to shine, bringing out the federal nature of our polity, a characteristic that is sadly under-emphasised in our strongly Union centric Constitution.

Karnataka has been chosen as a case study but similar arguments apply almost everywhere in India. Agitations for a separate Saurashtra, Vidarbha, Baghelkhand, Harit Pradesh, Kongu Nadu, Gorkhaland and Bodoland are nearly as old as independence.

Uttar Pradesh is a standard example of a state that is so big that it has become unwieldy and inefficient. The case for division of this behemoth state was made by K. M. Panikkar, the chairperson of the 1955 States Reorganisation Commission. The same call was given by Kumari Mayawati when she was the chief minister of the state and Yogi Adityanath in the days before he became chief minister.

To give a telling example, if a state called Doab was created out of the narrow strip of land between the Ganga and the Yamuna roughly between Kannauj and Prayagraj, it would be larger than the 35th most populous country in the world.

To put it simply, India is too big to have just 28-and-odd states plus smaller Union Territories. Is it too unreasonable to ask for 75 smaller states in the Union of India as a gift we give ourselves on this 75th anniversary of our independence?

A nearly automatic response might be to say that more states would lead more easily to fragmentation and disintegration of the country. This might be true in a European nation-state like Yugoslavia and Czechoslovakia (where such a thing has indeed happened) but it is not true in a civilisational state like India. In India, unity flows from diversity and not the other way round. We are diverse in just about everything except the biggest of things and this is the unique strength of our country. Diversity in India is incompletely and improperly expressed in our present set-up of 28 states and eight UTs. The time for deep-seated change is now.

What in effect I am proposing with 75 states is a countrywide delimitation exercise that will incidentally empower small states economically to a considerable degree. India is a quasi-federation. Any federation works best when the sizes of the constituent units are equal. The number 75 suggests itself because each new state would have an entirely manageable number of two crore inhabitants. And such an exercise would also fit in well with the proposed expansion of the Lok Sabha. Each new state would have around 10 elected representatives. Such an exercise cannot be done piecemeal nor in response to agitations. It has to be done all at one go, supported by a national consensus on the matter.

It will also need to be accompanied by changes in the system of governance. The Westminster model which has never really suited us would become unmanageable and unwieldy with 75 states. The US system with its strict separation of legislative and executive wings of government and elected chief executives at the centre and in the states might be more appropriate for us.

Abolition of the Rajya Sabha and Legislative Councils, bodies that have been stridently opposed since the days of the Constituent Assembly (1946-1949), might also be timely. Many have felt that the Upper House is an anachronism and that it represents nothing and nobody, certainly not the states it is supposed to represent. I agree.

The creation of new states needs just Article 3 but this is insufficient and actually meaningless without accompanying changes in governance. This would need a new Constituent Assembly, not an unreasonable step, and one from which many other liberal democracies have not shied away.

Our Constitution is not an immutable holy book. It is a man-made volume and it is capable of being changed by other men and women from a newer age to better reflect the aspirations of an India of the future.

> *A few months after "Bhārat: India 2.0" was released I felt the need for another supporting article. Once again I stress the lopsided sizes of our 28 states. Clearly I am thinking about the problems that this mismatch of sizes will create in the delimitation exercise that was looming three years down the line, that is in 2026. Now I have written a book on delimitation, and 2026 is nearly upon us now. Quo vadis?*

India with 75 states Will Lead to Optimized Growth and Development

The Sunday Guardian, 4 March 2023

Ideally, one could have 75 states with a population of roughly 2 crore each.

With India's burgeoning population, socio-economic and socio-political challenges staring at us, there is now an increasing sense of acceptance that states in the country are too large to ensure optimal governance for their potential growth and development.

The average constituent federal unit in Switzerland (canton) and the United States (state) has 3 lakh and 66 lakh inhabitants, respectively. In India it is a whopping 4.92 crore. For purely administrative convenience it is advantageous therefore to have small states with considerable devolution of powers within a state.

At the time of Independence, India consisted of fairly large provinces of the erstwhile British India and a motley collection of smaller and larger Princely States, around 550 in all. Thanks to Vallabhbhai Patel, all these were placed on the same constitutional footing, save one. It was clear that this hotchpotch would need to be modified and possibly this was the reason why Article 3 was phrased in the way it was. Reorganization of state boundaries was made a fairly simple business and lay in the hands of Parliament alone.

The States Reorganization Commission (1955) did the first major job in redrawing the boundaries of states, although the process began, in the case of Andhra Pradesh, as early as 1953. Subsequent demarcations were largely a result of agitations, demands and movements for the formation of smaller states which were held to be more representative of people's aspirations.

Interestingly, Andhra Pradesh which was the first state to be carved out on linguistic lines was also the first non-Hindi speaking state to be bifurcated in 2014 with the creation of Telangana. In 1956, language was a sufficient marker of identity; by 2014 it was deemed to be unnecessary.

There is a good case for smaller states in terms of the economy. There are also sound geographical, historical, cultural, geostrategic and administrative reasons for making smaller states. These reasons draw on the rich diversity of our country. Diversity is what characterizes India. It is our strongest point. We need smaller states because only then can true diversities emerge and flourish. Any aspirational nation is proud of its assets and as a consequence its citizens positively feel to be part of a larger endeavour. In India, we have unfortunately tended to highlight our weaknesses—be they religious divides, caste identities or linguistic chauvinisms.

The reflexive counter-argument is that smaller states would result in balkanization and disruption of the country. Others would argue that having, say, 75 states would make the Union government oppressively powerful to the detriment of state identity. Both arguments are contestable. They might be valid in a nation state like Czechoslovakia, Yugoslavia, USSR or the Austro-Hungarian and Ottoman empires. They are not true in a civilizational state where identifying distinctive characteristics of small population groups would only make them all feel a part of being under a big canopy of Bhāratavarsha, a concept that transcends religion, caste and creed. What one is arguing for is essentially a new Constitution that better measures true diversity in this vast land. Ideally, one could have 75 states with a population of roughly 2 crore each.

States have the major responsibility of providing healthcare, education, grassroots governance and law enforcement. In a working federation, states should be in a position to generate adequate finances to undertake these responsibilities and the freedom to spend the money they generate without interference from the Centre. The Centre should restrict itself to just matters of strategic, security and national importance, namely, defence, external affairs, communications, taxation and currency management along with formulation of broad fiscal policy. In this case it would be doing what any Union government should be doing and restricting itself to only that. India needs economically strong states and a politically strong Centre. What we have now sadly enough seems to be the reverse.

Smaller states can definitely be leveraged economically. In a recent book, I have suggested the outlines of 75 states and I will select four of them—Kashmir, Kutch, Kongu Nadu and Kashi—to illustrate this point. Kashmir can be made a hub for value-added products, from saffron to lavender and rose, allowing it to compete advantageously with Bulgaria, Iran and Spain. Kutch, with its low population, dry weather and sunny climate is the ideal location to become the solar energy nucleus for India and be compared to Israel in this regard. Kongunadu can similarly overtake Bangladesh in the textile and garment industry, while Kashi, incorporating the Bhojpuri speaking areas of eastern UP and Western Bihar, can easily be made into a cultural capital of the world that rivals, say Vatican City in terms of its tourism revenues. Smaller states can concentrate on their niche areas, thereby generating large revenues to use for day-to-day needs of their people. If states are given enough freedom by the Centre to generate and spend their revenues, we have the makings of 75 economic powerhouses in India.

A natural corollary to the formation of small states is the complete separation of legislative and executive wings of government at both Central and State levels, largely like in the US. It is interesting to note that our Constituent Assembly did consider the US Constitution briefly. Why it did not adopt the same can only remain a matter of speculation, but one could believe that we defaulted into the Westminster model simply because we were a British colony. This model anyway becomes unworkable with 75 states.

What these matters need is a thorough discussion in public forums, in a non-emotional way. The natural genius and talents of Indians do not find their full expression if one examines the state of our country 75 years after Independence. Would it be unreasonable then to say that the basic template of our governance structure needs reconsideration?

"Bhārat: India 2.0", Vitasta Publications, New Delhi (2022) attempts to shed more light on these matters.

> *Mischievous comments on India not being a nation but a "union of states" parleying as equals in some sort of negotiated settlement in 1947 began to emerge from the ranks of the opposition. Even more disturbingly, aspects of sovereignty were being ascribed to some states headed by regional parties. The word 'sovereignty' is a serious one and misusing it, as one opposition party was doing, carried with it grave implications. I wondered what some parties would not do to win an election. We wrote this following article quickly and possibly it reflects my agitation.*

Sovereignty, State, and Nation

Swarajya, 10 May 2023

The organic and essential basis of the Indian State is constituted of popular sovereignty, the indivisibility of India, and parliamentary supremacy. Rather suddenly, this somewhat exotic word 'sovereignty' has assumed center stage in Indian politics. Both the Congress party and BJP have invoked it during the Karnataka campaign; the former rather alarmingly terming a constituent state of India as 'sovereign', followed by the latter, led by PM Narendra Modi, sharply rebutting this description.

Almost uncannily, a new "sovereign" was crowned in far away England during the same time.

What exactly does it mean to term something, or someone, as 'sovereign'? Or does this word merely refer to a ceremonial gold coin, with the profile of this above-mentioned monarch and his ancestors? One might even see this quaint coin here and there in India today, weighing all of 8g of 22 carat gold!

At its most basic level, the word 'sovereignty' means supremacy: of power, of will, and of unquestionable writ.

The word almost implies purity derived from strength. What is sovereign is irreproachable, and unshakeable; sovereignty is both the might of a country as well as the foundation from which this might arises. In a political context, sovereignty is associated only with a country.

The Congress's description of Sonia Gandhi's speech, thus, was a secessionist slogan which claims that there exists a Karnataka devoid of India, which may do as it pleases.

It is not possible that this statement was tweeted by her party's official handle with gusto, without prior application of mind. A word pregnant with constitutional meaning should not be thrown about in a language which only the elite of this country understands. The statement is not just a deliberate disturbance, but an insight into what the tukde tukde gang wish to do to India.

By no means was this statement out of the blue. Rahul Gandhi, the disqualified former MP, had recently given his own nefarious spin to India being a "Union of States". In his view, nothing more than India's sundry states exist, and 'India' in his view is a ramshackle agglomeration of the same, our millenia old civilizational continuity be damned. He even spoke about a continuing "negotiation" between his 'union' and his 'states', as if the two can be held as equals.

How can such utterances not be intentional? Unsurprisingly, the well-known gaggle of irritants and saboteurs of this country parrot Churchill, when he had dismissed all of Indian civilization along with its terrific history of resilience in the face of invasions by declaring that "India is a geographical term. It is no more a united nation than the equator." Even though the British have long left our shores, this ideology appears embedded in this country's institutions.

It is indeed true that India is a Union of states: an indivisible, indestructible, ancient Union, Bhāratavarsha, which has, from time to time, arranged itself into smaller subdivisions.

Today, post 1947, these subdivisions are known as states. Many states which existed as on 15 August 1947 are but faint memories, and many states have emerged as novel constructions based on the Union's wisdom conjoined with local demands.

Any student of India's Constitution knows that with the operational simplicity of Article 3, states can be created, merged, reduced, made into Union Territories, or even made to disappear, at the behest of Parliament, regardless of the wishes of the state itself; whither 'sovereignty' when your very existence is beholden to a higher power, i.e. the Union?

To call India federal is an imperfect analogy at best, even incorrect, hence the "quasi" appendage is often tagged on to it. India is what it is, and descriptions, arising from a Western lens, and which try to cope ineffectually with India's unique civilisational setup, cannot be allowed to define what or who we are.

While India and the Indian civilisation have persisted in the face of repeated attacks, they are being summarily dismissed by the upper echelons of India's largest opposition party.

For petty electoral concerns and a galaxy of vested interests, domestic and foreign, the beautiful diversities within the country which are products of a timeless civilization, are being deformed into fault lines of a type that have weakened India before in its long history, with devastating consequences. Naturally, these tukde-tukde gangs are the same people who have consternation writ large on their faces when the cry of "Bharat Mata ki jai" resounds.

The makers of the Constitution had utmost clarity when they discussed what sovereignty meant in the Indian context. Acharya J. B. Kriplani, a member of the Constituent Assembly, asserted: "it is necessary to lay down clearly and distinctly, that sovereignty resides in and flows from the people." The same statement found resonance with Bhimrao Ambedkar, when he said: "I say that this Preamble embodies what is the desire of every Member of the House that this Constitution should have its root, its authority, its sovereignty, from the people. That it has."

The Rashtra is what lends authority to, organizes, and vests power into the Rajya. At the most fundamental level, and as voiced by the people who engineered our Constitution, this is the foundational and overriding dictum.

Unfortunately, the long rule of Macaulay's spoilt children is what is responsible for the destabilizing decrees coming not just from the Gandhi-Vadras, but the broader Lutyens leftist disruptionist ecosystem, including some opposition governments in larger states. The governmental institutions of this country, the interpretation of the Constitution, and how we understand rights and duties are far removed from the civilizational ontology which is the very basis for the noble edifice of this country.

A system of law flowing from distant England, peppered with whatever new Western fad with which the elite of this country are currently flirting, ensures that the voices of the true and only sovereigns of India, the people of this country, are consistently suppressed.

In the name of protecting democracy, the popular will (which democracy ought to subserve) is often lampooned, discredited, or outright ignored by those who think they know better, based on the crispness of their English accents, their Lahori kebabs, or their lavish Ghazal soirees.

Parts of the Rajya, which includes not just the State apparatus but all institutions which influence decision-making, have even shown outright hostility and contempt for the Rashtra. Certain individuals, platforms, and cliques in this country have come to view themselves as sovereign. Why is the State silent? Above all, it should be the State that is the most sensitive to encroachments on its sovereignty.

These tukde-tukde entities understand that their intoxication with power can only continue if they continuously keep attacking the

Rashtra, denigrate the civilizational basis for this country, and maintain India in a divided, disorderly state. Hence, The Kashmir Files or The Kerala Story receive sudden and acerbic backlash from repeat offenders, who go as far as to condone violence against it or ban it outright.

They wish to take us back to the pre-2014 era, where corruption and mismanagement fueled debauchery in gated environs, while 'coalition dharma' would override rajdharma. Even foreign policy was not spared; anything concerning Sri Lanka would be held ransom to the vagaries of the DMK, an essential coalition partner in the hotchpotch waterloo of indecision known as the UPA-2.

The fault, unfortunately, lies at the doors of the makers of the Constitution. They presumed that something so sacrosanct a postulate as the supremacy of the people of India, and hence its will, would never be questioned. They could have never foreseen the oddity of judicial inventions such as the basic structure doctrine, nor could they have predicted the greed of their political successors.

The Constitution, thus, does not emphasise or even talk about the organic and essential basis of the Indian State: popular sovereignty, the indivisibility of India, and parliamentary supremacy.

A brief perusal of the Constitution Assembly Debates is sufficient proof that all of these elements were inseparable from the Constitution—in the words of its makers—no less.

The foundational scheme of the Constitution itself is found lacking in this regard.

As India hurtles towards a century of independence, the fact that statements such as those made by the Gandhi-Vadras go unpunished is deeply distressing. Even administratively, the British-era Government of India Act, 1935, forms the backbone of the Constitution—a scheme which has long outlived its utility. If 105 amendments cannot fix it, nothing will; with all due respect, for the sake of the Rashtra, a new constitutional scheme appears to be an imperative.

A Constitution in a civilizational State such as India ought to carry instructions from the Rashtra to the Rajya. The bare basics of the organization of the Rajya, the overriding values which it must serve, and a charter of duties to enforce as well as the rights it ought to ensure should be the essentials of any decent Constitution.

The organization of the State, in particular, has to be in line with the civilizational characteristics of the Rashtra. If only the present Constitution had exercised abundant caution, the Rashtra would have been able to effectively respond and deter those who dare to subvert the unity and continuity of this civilization. A Dharmic Constitution, where Dharma and the popular mandate are enshrined as non-negotiable, is the natural starting point for the conversation. What that may look like is explored in the book "Bhārat: India 2.0" by Gautam R. Desiraju (Vitasta, 2022).

> *The crux of the above article is found in the short paragraph that says: The Rashtra is what lends authority to, organizes, and vests power into the Rajya. At the most fundamental level, and as voiced by the people who engineered our Constitution, this is the foundational and overriding dictum.*
>
> *I repeated some of these arguments six months later. Sometimes it becomes necessary to do this for the idea to sink deeply enough in the minds of people. There is some current discussion on why centralization is not such a good idea. I disagree with this tenet. We still need another decade of centralization so that the core of Bhārat is strengthened.*

State Reorganization and Centralization: A Deep Dive

Swarajya, 11 November 2023

Summary: Why it's necessary to repeatedly emphasize that India is a union, and not a federation.

Bhārat is a large and diverse country, and has been divided for mostly administrative reasons into a number of states. These states have been created, dissolved and divided by Parliament using the provisions of the all-important Article 3 of the Indian Constitution which states that, "Parliament may by law (a) form a new state by separation of territory from any state or by uniting two or more states or parts of states or by uniting any territory to a part of any state; (b) increase the area of any state; (c) diminish the area of any state; (d) alter the boundaries of any state; (e) alter the name of any state.

This means that the Central government can, without reference to any of the concerned states it has created by the provisions of this very Article, recreate, dissolve or divide these states. This Article also underlines the fact that Bhārat, that is India, is a Union of states and not a Federation.

The term 'Union' has a distinctive meaning in the Constitution and signifies that our states had no specific characteristic or feature, as on 15 August 1947, which suggested any kind of autonomy, far less sovereignty. At the time of independence, India consisted of the provinces of British India and, next, the Princely States. The former were created purely for administrative and other conveniences by the colonial power. Orissa and Bihar were separated from Bengal, and Sind from Bombay, for example. Burma and Ceylon were even detached completely from the Indian Empire in the early 20th century.

It was well recognised by 1950 that the provinces and other parts of British India would need to be reconfigured in due course, which in part, led to Article 3 being framed the way it was. The three big presidencies of British India, namely Bengal, Bombay and Madras were very diverse in many matters and administratively very cumbersome to operate because they were far flung in terms of area. The Princely States were more compact and usually culturally and linguistically more uniform, although some large ones like Hyderabad and Kashmir were quite diverse in themselves. A reorganisation was clearly required and took place in stages, notably in 1956 and later in 1966; other changes in the boundaries of the North Eastern states took place even further down the line. The formation of Telangana from a larger Andhra Pradesh took place as recently as 2014. Sometimes, erstwhile Princely States or parts of them were merged with parts of British India to create a new state. Karnataka is a prime example. It includes the whole of princely Mysore, parts of princely Hyderabad, and parts of erstwhile Madras and Bombay presidencies.

This sort of arrangement in independent India where constituent states were created at the pleasure of the Central authority is very far from the mischievous interpretations given to the phrase "Union of states" by individuals like Rahul Gandhi and M. K. Stalin. The former, in a speech in Parliament, earlier this year said that, "India is described in the Indian Constitution as a union of states and not as a nation. One cannot rule over the people of a state in India. Different languages and cultures cannot be suppressed. It is a partnership, not a kingdom." By any objective standard, this statement is erroneous and misleading. Firstly, the comment that India is not a nation is absurd, even ludicrous. Further, India is not a kingdom with hereditary monarchs. Nobody is trying to suppress any language or regional identity. M. K. Stalin, clearly echoing the words of Rahul Gandhi, has his own interesting interpretation of the word "union" which is not the meaning intended in the Constitution.

Significantly, words like "federation" and "federal" do not figure in our Constitution. Above all, they do not appear in the Preamble. India is not a federation if one goes by the constitutionally accepted meaning of the word. A federation is a country where more or less sovereign States (notice the use of the capital 'S' here, to distinguish this word from the version we use with a small 's' signifying our 28 states that are but creatures of Parliament) come together and surrender some or all of their sovereignty for the common good of the bigger entity, the Federation. The U.S.A., Switzerland and Germany are textbook examples of a federation. The word "Union" was used in our Constitution to describe our country so as to distinguish us from a "Federation", which we are not.

Elements of federalism crept into our governance structures simply because of the great size and diversity of Bhārat. We have been described as being pseudo-federal, quasi-federal and so on. None of these definitions confer on our states the authority to do what they please in the name of language, caste, religion, diversity and culture. Above all, they do not give the right to any state to secede from the Union, a fact that should be well noted by some of our larger, more politically troublesome states that seem to think that they are exalted manifestations of some regional characteristic that stands higher than the national ethos. The recent statement by the son of the above mentioned M. K. Stalin about destroying Sanatana Dharma falls within this motley collection of false and destructive statements that seem to have no intent other than the complete break up of Bharat into innumerable pieces, simply to dislodge the Bharatiya Janata Party (BJP) from power at the Centre.

The Centre and the states have clearly demarcated responsibilities that are laid out in Schedule VII of our Constitution and these responsibilities are enumerated in the Central, State and Concurrent Lists that date from the colonial era and keep getting modified from time to time. Nobody rules over anybody in India, whatever be the manner in which Rahul Gandhi might choose to depict the situation. Possibly his statement has Freudian undertones of a wannabe Emperor of India ruling the country from Lutyens Delhi. His idea of a "partnership" between the Centre and the states is both misleading and mischievous.

Using tricks of the English language and the Tamil language, a picture is being painted of our 28 states (not to mention the Union Territory of Delhi) as being a number of sovereign entities parleying independently with the Centre to evolve a mutually agreeable arrangement for governance. This is very far from the truth. Our present Constitution is strongly weighted in favour of the Centre. B. R. Ambedkar himself recognised this, and approved. Above all, a strong Centre ensures national security, a robust defence setup and a uniform fiscal system. In the context of the first two points, the fact that large states like West Bengal, Maharashtra and Tamil

Nadu all have terrestrial or maritime international boundaries should not be lost on anyone. The consequences of too much decentralisation in say, the North East or in the Union Territories of Jammu & Kashmir and Ladakh are again all too obvious.

In this background, the BJP government's efforts to centralise power have been met with mixed reactions. Some have criticized the government for undermining the 'federal' structure of the Indian Constitution (whatever this might mean), while supporters of the Central government have argued that centralisation is necessary to ensure India's progress. Those who support the BJP government's centralisation efforts argue that it is necessary to address a number of challenges facing the country. The inevitable fact of the matter is that whenever a single party commands a majority in the Lok Sabha, power flows naturally to the Centre. This simple fact should be borne in mind by our several opposition parties who claim that the present set up is majoritarian. The parliamentary democracy system with first-past-the-post elections is by definition majoritarian. It is just that coalition governments have existed at the Centre for so long before 2014 that many have come to think of majoritarian governments as somehow being dictatorial, fascist and Nazi-like. Nothing could be further from the truth.

First, India is a large and diverse country, with a wide range of regional and cultural differences. A more balanced Centre-state power sharing approach can help to ensure that all regions of the country are treated fairly and that national policies are implemented effectively.

Second, centralisation can help to improve efficiency and reduce corruption. When there are multiple levels of government, there is a risk of duplication of effort and inefficiency. Centralisation can help to streamline government operations and make it easier to implement policies.

Third, centralisation can help to strengthen national security. In a centralised system, the central government has more control over the security forces and can coordinate their efforts more effectively. This can help to improve the country's ability to respond to threats, both internal and external.

The BJP government's centralisation efforts have already had a number of positive outcomes. For example, the National Investigation Agency (NIA) has been able to investigate and prosecute terrorist cases more effectively under the NIA (Amendment) Act, 2019. The government has also been able to crack down on terrorist organizations like the Popular Front of India (PFI) under the Unlawful Activities (Prevention) Amendment Act, 2019. Again, the Central Vigilance Commission (CVC) has been able to investigate corruption cases against state government officials more effectively under the CVC (Amendment) Act, 2021.

A study by the Centre for Policy Research (CPR) found that centralisation has been a key factor in India's economic growth since independence. The study found that states with higher levels of centralisation have grown faster than states with lower levels of centralisation.

Another study by the National Council of Applied Economic Research (NCAER) found that centralisation has helped to improve the delivery of public services in India. The study found that states with higher levels of centralisation have better performing public services than states with lower levels of centralisation. One might term this as the success of the 'double engine sarkar' at work.

While there is always the risk that centralisation could be used to suppress dissent and concentrate power in the hands of the central government, it is our considered opinion that the BJP central government, given its onerous responsibility in governing a vast, diverse country like Bharat, has so far used its powers responsibly. Nothing is perfect but the centrifugal impulses that originate from states where languages other than Hindi are spoken, are still too troublesome in terms of the ways in which such impulses may impact on national security and protection of our borders.

It is a measure of the responsible behaviour of the Central government with regard to its relations with the states that it has rarely invoked the draconian provisions of Articles 355 and 356 in the last nine years.

Centralisation is a necessary and positive development in India. The BJP government's centralisation efforts have helped to improve the delivery of public services. For example, the government's One Nation, One Ration Card scheme has made it easier for people to access food grains under the Public Distribution System, regardless of where they live in the country. The government's Pradhan Mantri Jan Dhan Yojana scheme has also helped to bring millions of people into the formal banking system.

Centralisation has also helped to promote economic development. For example, the government's Make in India initiative has helped to attract foreign investment and create new jobs in the country. The government's Goods and Services Tax (GST) has also helped to create a unified market in India, making it easier for businesses to operate across state borders. That the states have been given so much power in setting up norms for the collection of GST is another strong confirmation of a balanced Centre-state relationship.

As examples of autonomy given to states in countries with a responsible federal structure, one might mention Italy where the cultural and linguistic differences have been prevalent for a couple of centuries just like in the Indian subcontinent. For example, the Aosta Valley is an autonomous region in Italy that is home to a large French-speaking population. In the same way, South Tyrol (another autonomous region in northern Italy) has a large German speaking population. The region has its own government and legislature, and it is responsible for a wide range of matters, including education, healthcare, and taxation.

Another example is the state of Hawaii which is located offshore from the mainland U.S.A in the Pacific Ocean and is home to a diverse population of people from different ethnic and cultural backgrounds. The state has its own government and legislature, and it is responsible for a wide range of matters, including education, healthcare and environmental protection.

The population of India varies significantly from state to state. For example, Uttar Pradesh has a population of 241 million people, while Mizoram has just 1.3 million. This stark difference in population presents a number of challenges for the Indian government in terms of Centre-state relations, as it must try to ensure that all states have fair access to goods, facilities and services. A possible solution is to reconfigure the Rajya Sabha so that it has the same number of elected representatives from each state. The Senate in the U.S.A. with exactly two directly elected members from each state could be the model. The present Rajya Sabha structuring is based on indirect elections with a collegium and is far from satisfactory.

Overall, India's governance system is a unique one in that there are certain federal elements that have been shaped by the country's history, culture, and diversity. Our system has its own challenges, but it has also been successful in ensuring generally that all states in India have access to adequate resources and services. It is important that citizens become more aware of the nuances of Centre-state relations and avoid being misled by unscrupulous politicians in the run up to several Assembly elections and the all-important Lok Sabha election next year.

We've spoken again about the Rajya Sabha. Clearly this body and its near irrelevance to governance continues to trouble me. There is also a lot said about federalism. I feel it should be dinned into the minds of school children after they enter the higher secondary school that India is not a federation. A country is either a federation or not a federation. There is nothing in between. A woman cannot be half pregnant.

The next article is my first major salvo against the present 1950 constitution and its many amendments. Bibek Debroy raised the issue of a new constitution and this prompted me to write the piece that follows.

Does India Need a New Constitution?

Firstpost, 7 October 2023

Summary: A document that incorporates Bhārat's cultural and spiritual dimensions would more explicitly reinforce a sense of inclusivity and unity among its diverse population across religions, castes and languages.

A recent article by Bibek Debroy, Chairman of the Economic Advisory Council to the Prime Minister (EAC-PM) underlines the need for a new constitution for India if it is to become a world power by 2047. The author highlights issues such as the ideal number of states for effective governance, the need to examine the Seventh Schedule, judicial reform, the role of the all-India services, the relevance of the Rajya Sabha, and whether we need Part IV (Directive Principles of State Policy) at least in its present form. There is little doubt that it is his position as Chairman EAC-PM that has heightened interest in a subject that had till now lain on the back burner.

The crux of Debroy's argument for a new Constitution is that the present one closely parallels the Government of India Act 1935. Nearly 250 of the present 395 Articles in our 1950 Constitution have nearly exact equivalents in the 1935 Act, which was drawn up, in the end, by a colonial power and not by an independent sovereign State. It is not appreciated that the bulk of the present document was drafted not by B. R. Ambedkar, but by B. N. Rau, an ICS bureaucrat, who had earlier drafted similar documents for the British in 1946.

Ambedkar was, to be frank, just the chairman of the Drafting Committee, which contained many heavyweight legal luminaries. He was the first among equals.

It was nearly inevitable that the common features in all these prior documents literally defaulted India into its present mode of governance with its federal structure, distribution of powers between the Union and the States, a bicameral legislature (Lok Sabha and Rajya Sabha), three wings of government (executive, judiciary, legislature), the separation of powers between them, the roles of the President and the state Governors, emergency provisions, setting up of an Election Commission, the Union, State and Concurrent Lists, and above all, the parliamentary form of government with a first-past-the-post system of elections.

In short, the Constitution we chose in 1950 adopted several administrative structures and procedures from the Government of India Act 1935, mostly I suspect to ensure a smooth transition from colonial rule to democratic governance. But today, I ask the question, do we need this kind of evolutionary constitutional development? India is becoming Bharat today, and this is not an evolutionary change. It is a fundamental tectonic movement. We seem to finally know who we are. We are not the Indians of 1947 but the Bharatiyas of 2023. Does the 1950 Constitution, even given the steady guidance it has given us for 75 years, do full justice to us today? I think not.

The current constitution does not reflect the rich cultural, spiritual, and dharmic heritage of India. India is a very diverse country. Diversity is our strength. This diversity of Indian society and its deep-rooted spiritual traditions are not captured in a constitution that was so strongly influenced by colonial legal frameworks. Retaining the present Constitution, by invoking a blind worship of the past, overlooks the opportunity to enshrine the unique spiritual and cultural essence of India in our Vision Statement that is the Constitution.

A document that incorporates Bharat's cultural and spiritual dimensions would more explicitly reinforce a sense of inclusivity and unity among its diverse population across religions, castes and languages. A constitution that reflects our civilisational values would certainly reinforce a stronger sense of national identity. This is especially true today when the whole world is recognising that we are a civilisational state and not a nation state.

Proponents of retaining the present constitution might argue that its foundations have allowed for India's democratic and secular evolution over the years. They might believe that rather than replacing the entire constitution, it might be more practical to amend it strategically to better reflect India's cultural and spiritual dimensions. I refute such arguments. The word 'secular' itself has been fully discredited in India today, and by 'democracy' we should be enshrining our Bharatiya version of it rather than the Western liberal model, which we have been saddled with since 1950.

Still other questions remain apart from those pointed out by Debroy. Is a parliamentary democracy the best form of governance for us? Is first-past-the-post better than proportional representation? Should there be a complete separation of legislative and executive wings in other words, the American system? Would 75 small states work well in the latter situation? Can the Rajya Sabha be scrapped?

Constitutionally, we are at an inflection point today. The time of "soothing and baffling expedients, of delays" brought about with amendments and adjournments, is long since gone. "In its place we are entering a period of consequences," to quote someone we all love to hate, Winston Churchill.

Drafting a new Constitution will be a new exercise for us. It can be initiated only by the three wings of government, but having done so, they would then need to surrender a major part of their sovereignty to a Constituent Assembly that would need to be formed with care and concern. The 1946 Assembly was remarkably free of partisan rancour, possibly because at least 30 per cent of its membership consisted of apolitical figures drawn from various segments of public life. A Constituent Assembly is a sovereign body that stands apart and higher than Parliament, as Parliament cannot influence the drafting of a new Constitution. The judiciary cannot, by definition, have any role in reviewing the merits or otherwise of a new Constitution. But above all, and this would be paramount, the Executive wing should play no role at all in the drafting. Constitutions are written to stay around for some time. They should not reflect the immediate electoral priorities of political parties. The problems with our 1950 Constitution mostly arose because a generally reasonable document became distorted with the amendments during 1950-1980. These amendments were such that they suited the political preferences of the Congress Party, in particular Jawaharlal Nehru (after the Avadi meeting in 1955) and Indira Gandhi.

I am glad Debroy has brought up the matter of a new Constitution. A number of articles and podcasts have quickly surfaced in past weeks, including one featuring this author. More will emerge soon. This is because a new Constitution is an idea whose time has come.

Essays on Pakistan

My interest in Pakistan grew after I wrote a review of Venkat Dhulipala's magisterial work on Pakistan as a failed Medina in 2018. I showed my review to friends who were descended from Hindu families that had to migrate to India from West Punjab and East Bengal, the other side of silence, and all of them said that I had grasped the essential fact that the idea of Pakistan was doomed from the start. M. J. Akbar possibly had the last word when he said that "The idea of India is stronger than the Indian. The idea of Pakistan is weaker than the Pakistani". In many ways, my interest in Pakistan (which I visited in 2014) only stimulated my interest in the Constitution of India and, ironically therefore, it was Pakistan that made me write "Bhārat: India 2.0" in 2022, a book that depicts Bhārat as a civilizational state rather than as a European type nation-state. In this depiction, Pakistan was an artificial nation-state created by the British to preserve their geopolitical interest in the sub-continent, and not really a result of any systemic antipathy between Hindus and Muslims in undivided India—all this came later, after Partition.

No analysis of our constitution can be performed without discussing Partition because, in my view, our constitution itself is a reaction to Partition and was written in such a way that a second religion-based partition should not occur in the newly independent India: if this had happened, our very existence as a viable country would have come into question and people like Churchill would have had the last laugh.

Now, there are many theories as to why Pakistan, which was just a dream in the mind of Rahmat Ali in 1931, became a full fledged reality in just 16 years. Hindus and Muslims had lived in India for nearly 1000 years, maybe uneasily at times, but never till the 1930s did the Muslims feel that they needed a separate country where they would not need to live among Hindus. In large parts of India, Muslims constituted the ruling classes till the early 18th century. Possibly, they felt threatened after 1858 when Hindus took to English-based education and started obtaining low level government jobs in British India. Muslims possibly felt like second-class citizens after that, which is possibly the reason why the ideas of Syed Ahmed Khan and his founding of the Aligarh Muslim University obtained so much traction. It is no coincidence that AMU remained the intellectual capital of Islam in undivided India and that it was the crucible of Pakistan after the 1920s. Let us still not forget though that as late as 1946 a Unionist, anti-Partition coalition of Muslims, Hindus and Sikhs, won the assembly elections in Punjab, and that it was only a virtual guarantee by Jinnah to Punjabi Muslims that land reforms would not be effected in Pakistan that they swung to his side, making Pakistan a reality.

The British played a key role. Churchill boasted that Jinnah existed as the leader of subcontinent Muslims only because the British allowed him to play that role. He was, in the end, the useful idiot in the grim game being played by Britain and America to have a pivot in the sensitive northwestern fringe of undivided India—the Great Game being played in another age. The British wanted a client state in that area to spy on the rapidly growing Soviet Union. Some say that all they wanted was a way to prevent uranium, mined in Tibet, reaching Kazakhstan in the U.S.S.R., and thereby hinder the Soviet atomic energy program. For this all they needed was territory in Gilgit, Chitral and Baltistan. The NWFP was just a useful add-on and in turn Punjab and Sind. The latter was convenient because it gave the British a toehold to Karachi, which they ran almost till the 1960s.

The British probably felt that a newly independent India under the leadership of Nehru, with his mild socialistic and leftist leanings could never be used as a client to spy on the Soviet Union. So India would have to be partitioned. This was the thinking as far back as the early 1940s with the then Viceroy, Linlithgow playing an active role in increasing the profile of Jinnah, the British puppet, as a leader of Indian Muslims. Ambedkar, Rajendra Prasad and Rajagoplachari all knew by then that Partition was an inevitability, and it must have been galling for them to contend with the likes of Gandhi and Nehru, who were resisting the idea of Pakistan. And so Jinnah got his 'plot of land' and proceeded to promptly die a year later.

The geography of Pakistan is unbelievably unsustainable for a sovereign nation. It is long and thin, with no strategic depth longitudinally. It is completely sustained by the waters of the Sindhu—the choke point that India has correctly identified as Pakistan's Achilles heel post Sindoor in 2025. All that it has is a strategically placed northern area in the mountains and warm water access in the south. All it has done is to rent out its geography, its people and its resources to the highest bidder. It is a classical example of a rentier state. To my mind it is not a country. Perhaps one could call it a negation of India.

With the decline of Britain as a world power after WW2 and especially after Suez, the USA rose nearly automatically to the pole position it occupies in world affairs till the present time. Custody of Pakistan passed from Britain to America. Pakistan has been unusually lucky as a client state. The Afghan-Soviet conflict in the 1980s and the World Trade Center destruction in 2001 provided it the opportunity to be anointed by the USA as a frontline defender of anti-terrorist actions. Everyone turned a blind eye to the fact that Pakistan was also using the largesse it was getting from America to train terrorists to cause havoc on the Indian side of the LOC in Jammu & Kashmir and also elsewhere in our country. The idea of good terrorists (freedom fighters) and bad terrorists (terrorists) also took hold in the American media and Pakistan benefited enormously. A third lucky break for Pakistan came when China started coveting the warm water port of Gwadar as a way in which it could escape the Malacca Straits chokepoint through which most of its oil supplies from the Gulf is routed.

The history of Pakistan over the past 80 or so years has been nothing but an unmitigated tragedy for Bhārat. As Atal Behari Vajpayee said one can choose one's friends but not one's neighbours. But there is a caveat here: what if one remakes one's neighbour so that it becomes not just one neighbour but three or four neighbours? This is the poser that I put forward in one of my most recent articles.

I wrote nearly ten or so short articles on Pakistan over the last seven or so years. I am confident about its imminent break up even as America and China lose interest in it, or have neither the stamina or money to keep it going longer than a few more years. For both countries Pakistan is no longer 'paisa vasool'. My guess is as good as yours, dear reader, and I don't give this strange country any further than 2028, for a complete de jure breakup into several small countries.

For Bhārat, no lasting peace and security is possible till it resolves the unresolved issues of Partition on both its western and eastern flanks for only this would render any meaning to the descriptor 'Bhāratavarsha'.

Jinnah was upset that the Pakistan he got in 1947 was "maimed, mutilated and moth-eaten". No one asks if the India we got in 1947 was also not "maimed, mutilated and moth-eaten". I am strongly of the opinion that unless and until we take back the territories we lost in 1947, or at least carve them into client buffer states, say Sindhu Desh, Balochistan and Pakhtunistan (greater Afghanistan), there will be no real peace in the Indian subcontinent, that is Bharatavarsha.

The following article seems tongue in cheek but raises again the question of what a nation-state is and this in turn begs the question as to what a nation is.

Unstable Boundaries: A Holiday Trip to Quetta or Peshawar, Anyone?

Swarajya, 8 March 2019

History is full of instances where political boundaries were drawn and erased. So it would hardly be a surprise if you plan a holiday to Peshawar, Quetta or Kabul in 10 years' time with just about the nonchalance that you would employ to go to Patna, Quilon or Kolhapur.

Cultural, social and linguistic characteristics of various peoples are shaped over centuries and are typically of a long term nature. Political boundaries, on the other hand, are man-made and are drawn or erased by the victors after major wars and conflicts. However, if the events of the past 150 years are any indication, these man-made political boundaries do not seem to have much shelf life in general. They are actually surprisingly ephemeral.

A look at the map of Europe over the last 100 years reveals this admirably. The First World War saw the end of four huge empires: the Habsburgs in Austria-Hungary, the Hohenzollerns in Germany, the Romanovs in Russia and the Ottomans in Turkey. Germany, however, bloated under Hitler to an enormous size by the early 1940s and with its vassal states controlled almost all of the European land mass. The end of the Second World War put an end to all this.

There were two Germanys of postage stamp size by 1945, and divided by a fundamental ideological conflict. The Union of Soviet

Socialist Republics (USSR) and its satellite states dominated much of Central Europe and all of Eastern Europe. But these political differences were not of fundamental importance. The idea of Germany was more important than all of this and the old fault lines reasserted themselves so that we now have the Europe of 2019 with a unified Germany as its fulcrum again even if it is not of its 1914 size. One USSR became 15 or so different countries. So much for communism.

Even more amazing than all this is the number of times the British have drawn and erased such boundary lines during the last century all over the world. It is almost their default mode of governance when things go wrong. They began with their own country and carved up Ireland in 1921. They created a string of artificial countries like Iraq, Jordan, Israel, Palestine, Yugoslavia and Czechoslovakia. Some have lasted uncomfortably, while others have vanished without a trace. The list is practically endless. It would be ironic if their own realm is divided as an outcome of Brexit. Anything can happen. We could have four countries where there is just one.

But going back to the past, their crowning glory was absolutely their 'Jewel in the Crown'. Ceylon and Burma were first lopped off from the rest of the Indian subcontinent. Finally came their magnum opus, the two headed Pakistan. One head was chopped off by India in 1971 showing the whole world the hollowness of their two nation theory—there were more Muslims in India compared to either Pakistan or Bangladesh.

The rest of Pakistan, the other head as it were, is tottering now as recent events are showing. Sindh, Balochistan and Khyber Pakhtunkhwa are all seething with separatist movements, the strongest of these being in Balochistan. The northwest of India and its environs in Central Asia have always been tempestuous and have been subjected to powerful undercurrents of history because this region lies in the fault lines of three powerful states: Russia, India and China. The Great Game of the late nineteenth century is a typical example of these undercurrents as is the Afghanistan and Iraq problems over the last several decades.

The smaller countries that lie at the junctions of these huge empires come and go: for example, all the xyz-stans. All these –stans are buffer states of the big three and are influenced one way or the other by them, and also by the underlying threads of the ancient Silk Route. This is what is permanent — not the political boundaries of today.

Given today's situation in Pakistan, it is not so difficult to sketch how the region might look in say, 2024 and this is what I have attempted. If the past 100 years are any indication, rearrangement of map lines could cascade quite suddenly, if other events favour such a development. The situation is metastable: a resurgent and economically strong India; a China with a flagging economy and a desire not to push India too far or too hard, and finally a Russia that wishes to antagonise neither India nor China. What are the buffer states in such a scenario? Nothing. Absolutely nothing.

My conjecture is not new and has been discussed on and off by people who surely know a whole lot more than me. I am merely a scientist. I have sketched this possibility as I would a reaction mechanism — based on existing facts and the known behavioural patterns of countries and individuals. As eminent a person as Dr Subramanian Swamy has suggested this for sometime now as a favourable policy strategy for India, and he is surely aware of the geopolitical and strategic niceties and is also well aware of the capabilities of India to play a crucial catalytic role in such a transformation with Balochistan surely being an incendiary point.

All this is in the realm of the believable. A look at the famous Brandenburg Gate in the heart of Berlin before and after the collapse of communism is revealing. I crossed Checkpoint Charlie in 1978 and saw the passport controls, guard dogs and barbed wire. The next time I visited Berlin was in 1990 and again in 1991 and I strolled through the very same gate with a friend eating an ice cream. So don't be surprised if you are able to plan a holiday to Peshawar, Quetta or Kabul in 10 years' time with just about the nonchalance that you would employ to go to Patna, Quilon or Kolhapur.

> *This was written in 2019. I said Pakistan would break up by 2024. It is now 2025. Pakistan has not broken up as yet. But it sure looks like that it is well on the way to splitting. The question really is not if but when.*
>
> *I waited four years before I wrote about Pakistan again. There is something like saying something correct too early. No one wants to listen to you. Either they don't need to or they don't understand you. Too many people were clinging to an old line that a stable Pakistan was good for India.*

Pakistan Requiem

The Sunday Guardian, 8 October 2023

Summary: In just a few years, the physical disintegration of Pakistan has become a distinct possibility.

The contrast between the two countries whose borders were cleaved by the Radcliffe line 75 years ago could not be less striking. While one side is racing towards becoming the world's third largest economy, the other side has descended into a rudderless morass which is incapable of enforcing its sovereign writ over the territories cartographically ascribed to it. Pakistanis question today whether they were ever masters of their own destiny, or mere playthings for powers indifferent, malicious, and everything in between.

In just a few years, the physical disintegration of Pakistan has become a distinct possibility, being grimly analysed by serious names worldwide, including within Pakistan. The country's demise is a result of its festering, insuperable internal contradictions violently reacting with the portentous changes underway in the world. The Covid-19 pandemic, the Taliban storming to power in Afghanistan, the fallout of the Ukraine war, India's increasing geopolitical clout, and Pakistan's febrile political meltdown have exposed the limitations inherent in its rentier state model. Pakistan's socio-political dynamics are in an unforeseen tailspin, while the economy is in tatters.

In 2023, it is impossible not to question the very basis of Pakistan's creation. Its formation sounds irrational, and quixotic, even comical to all of us Bharatiyas; it is an artificial flight of fancy which has descended into an unending nightmare for its own denizens. Pakistan is still the only country so formed when a religious minority separated from the majority. The oddities of such a conception were apparent from the get go, for a greater number of this minority continued to remain in the mother country. A body blow to the Two Nation Theory also came in 1971, when the country was sawn in half and their common religion was insufficient to hold them together. Further, Pakistan remains just a thin strip of land with no strategic depth consisting of seven distinct nationalities—Punjabi, Sindhi, Baloch, Pashtun, Kashmiri, Balti and Shina.

The ones who benefitted the most from this saga, apart from the British, were a select group of rich landowners and business families premised on the assurance that land reforms would remain stillborn. This very landowning class then came to enter into a symbiosis with the country's outsized army to give rise to an extractive rentier state which is by, for, and of 70-odd families. These families form the skeletal frame of the amorphous being called the "establishment" in Pakistani politics. The economic model of Pakistan has thus remained stagnant—rent out its army, its geographic location, and now its armaments.

With buyers no longer willing, Pakistan is at a loss—no global power has any reason to burn billions of dollars to bankroll Pakistan anymore, with America's war in Afghanistan ending and China's ambitions of CPEC practically kaput. Domestically, the imminent promise of Ghazwa-i-Hind after reconquering Kashmir from infidels allowed the army to manufacture consent, but with the army itself being hated after their misadventure with Imran Khan, disillusionment reigns.

The civilizational reawakening underway in India, partially emerging from the confidence of a strengthening economy, has made youngsters think more about Pakistan in context of their own heritage. Is the feeling of nationhood in Bhārat higher than sectarian adherence? Should one not question the motives of the principal players, be they Hindus, Muslims or Britishers? Were they thinking about India, or were they merely politicians, playing political games? Was Radhakrishnan correct when he said that Indians had allowed themselves to be divided by the British? Perhaps partition had more to do with British interests—maintaining control over the Indian Ocean and preventing the Soviets from accessing Gilgit's uranium and sharing a border with India. We are all watching recent Pakistani podcasts with wry amusement. In one, I heard a common man on the street saying that all that Jinnah got was a free plot of land, following which he promptly died.

Pakistan is like an ICU patient with multi-organ failure. The phenomenon of collapse seems to be less a question of if, and more a question of when and how. Major fissures are clearly identifiable. The first of course is an unviable economy; no tranches of IMF money can keep Pakistan afloat with the insatiable greed of the army and the ruling classes—the 70 families. The second could be an ethnic disturbance originating in the Pashtun communities in Khyber Pakhtunkhwa and Afghanistan's machinations as they try to establish an autonomous Pashtunistan, finally removing (in their eyes) the shame of the Durand line. An independent Balochistan is the wish of many in that province but its very small population makes this a less likely possibility. Gilgit-Baltistan and Pakistan Occupied Kashmir (PoK) with their Shia-Sunni divides are other flash points, now that people on the Pakistan side of undivided Jammu & Kashmir are more than ever aware of the better living standards of their compatriots across the LoC. India, on its part, has been sending signals that retaking PoK may be on the cards. Notably, the Pakistani Taliban (with their Afghan compatriots' blessings) have had recent skirmishes in the strategic area of Chitral, over which India has a legal claim. This area, if it returns to India, would provide a vital land link to Afghanistan and Central Asia. Punjab, the rump, is no longer united as sufficient fault lines seem to be developing between north and south Punjab.

To conclude, there seem to be but two outcomes for Pakistan—it lingers as a single country for a few more years with intermittent monetary infusions but with its peripheries escaping its reach, à la Syria or Lebanon. The second is that it undergoes Balkanization, with Gilgit-Baltistan and PoK making a natural reversion to India, as would be legally allowed by the international community. The attitudes and priorities of the United States, and to a lesser extent China and India, or even Saudi Arabia and the UAE, would determine which of these outcomes would actually occur. India's stance and behaviour in the event of a break-up of Pakistan is yet another question especially if we are confronted with a large number of refugees. Indeed, we live in interesting times.

> *After the farce of the 2024 Pakistan election, I could not resist writing this article. There is something deliciously horrible about this 'humsaya' of ours!*

Pakistan: Poised on a Knife's Edge

CNN News 18, 29 November 2024

Summary: The recent incidents have shown that any fig leaf of pretence that Pakistan had as a parliamentary democracy has also been done away with.

Pakistan has always been a strange country, if one could even ever call it that. Conjured out of thin air in the clerical Deobandi schools of western UP in the 1930s, infused with a fake sense of history and entitlement conjured in the Aligarh Muslim University around the same time, midwifed by the British for geostrategic interests of their own in the 1940s, and assiduously pampered by the Americans as their periscope into the USSR during the 1950s, this artificial nation-state received two more fortuitous leases on life: first, due to the Soviet invasion of Afghanistan, and second, because of the 9/11 attack on the World Trade Centre Twin Towers in New York City.

In each case, Pakistan received huge amounts of money from America (read US deep state) that was neatly stashed away by the generals who have ruled the country since 1957. This money has been funnelled into either a massive $100 billion business empire within Pakistan or into lavish residences, primarily in London. Despite being a nation of approximately 236 million people, Pakistan effectively serves the interests of only around 70 elite families who dominate its institutions.

Pakistan is well known as an army with a country attached. Governance, if one can refer to it by this name, has consisted of the army toying with puppet groups, purporting to be political parties and fomenting tribal divisions. This circus has been interspersed with bouts of outright martial law. Civilian prime ministers have been selected by the army, rather than being elected in a normal procedure that is followed by other democracies.

Only the US deep state calls Pakistan a democracy and much of the recent chaos and turmoil is the outcome of the latest experiment that this unfortunate country tried with democracy in February 2024. Whatever be the ills and idiosyncrasies of Imran Khan (and there are many), it is practically acknowledged that the election was stolen from undoubtedly the most popular politician in Pakistan, even as he has languished in various prisons since May 2023.

In such a scenario, the common people have remained wretchedly poor (and getting poorer with relentless inflation), and anyone with the slightest ability and capacity to do so has emigrated. The problems of the country are gigantic. It is overpopulated, and its main agricultural lifeline—the Sindhu River—is hopelessly silted, leaving the country prone to disastrous flooding. A primarily agricultural country, it does not have the capability of feeding its own people.

It has been in a precarious situation economically for a decade as the clientelist and rentier doles from America (and lately China) have practically dried up. As a consequence, it has settled over the last two years at a very low level of economic equilibrium, at an enormous cost to the common man. It practically exists today at the whim of the IMF, (read US deep state) and the Democratic Party in that country.

Culturally, Pakistan is fractured by deep fault lines among its four provinces—Punjab, Sindh, Khyber Pakhtunkhwa (KP), and

Baluchistan. These provinces differ vastly in size, population, and resources, with Punjab dominating the country. This dominance is deeply resented by the inhabitants of the other three provinces, who fear Punjab, especially as the army elite is predominantly drawn from there.

At the time of Partition, these provinces shared little in common except for being Muslim-majority and geographically contiguous—hardly a workable criterion for the formation of a new country. The parallels with the erstwhile Yugoslavia and Czechoslovakia, two other artificial creations of the West, are all too apparent. Neither of these two creations lasted longer than 70 years. Are the bells tolling for Pakistan?

The economic, social, cultural and ethnic contradictions are too many. The only factor that kept this show going was American money. American interest in Pakistan has, however, dwindled in the past few years. The Chinese also probably feel that Pakistan is not *paisa vasool*, not that their interest in Pakistan went beyond the Port of Gwadar and the road connecting it to the Trans-Karakoram highway, which is now practically a dead issue. Their secondary objective was to use Pakistan as an irritant against India, another strategy that has proven largely ineffective given India's growing stature and China's own economic woes and tensions with America.

Both America and China are probably exploring the possibility of limiting their labours to small zones of interest where local elites can be negotiated with, through outposts, mercenaries, and quasi-colonies.

Science tells us that unstable, multivariate and unpredictable systems go from what one deems complex to what is referred to as chaotic. A complex system is affected by many factors but the interplay between these factors is often understandable, once one recognises that the system is complex.

To use an analogy from international affairs, the present Ukraine war is a complex system as it involves primarily Russia and Ukraine, but the involvement of America, Europe and even India and the Middle East is palpable. If the war involved exclusively Russia and Ukraine, one would call it a simple system. However, many other countries are involved and so it becomes a complex system. But after two years, the Ukraine matter is largely predictable to all the actors. The only unknown now is how the war will end, but even here, one appreciates that it will be through negotiations between two men—Vladimir Putin and Donald Trump.

A chaotic system on the other hand is highly dynamic, unlike a complex system that is largely static. Dynamical means that the system is highly sensitive to initial conditions, which means that small changes in the starting state can lead to vastly different outcomes over time. Translating into layman's terms, whether an agitation begins in Baluchistan or KP can lead to widely different consequences for Pakistan —one scenario might lead to the country's breakup, while the other might not.

In other words, even minute differences in input can lead to significant changes in the system's evolution. Scientifically, chaos is not synonymous with randomness but rather it reflects deterministic unpredictability.

Pakistan today is still deterministic and not random. It will evolve over the next few months according to specific rules, but these rules are not known to anyone including the Pakistanis and their patrons. The specific rules in this case could be that there might be some negotiation between the two implacable enemies, Imran Khan and the army. But since we do not know when and how these negotiations will happen, the behaviour appears random. Complexity has become chaotic.

At the time of writing, the PTI, Imran Khan's party, has marched towards Islamabad demanding his release, claiming his life is at risk if he remains in jail any longer. However, the army cannot afford to release Khan, knowing that once freed, he would relentlessly target them. After all, the army remains Pakistan's oldest and most stable institution.

Hushed whispers in and around Rawalpindi also suggest that the army is indeed a divided house, which is far more faction-ridden than ever before. If there is no army, there is no Pakistan, so what kind of country does Khan hope to preside over? Would it be a fragmented hotchpotch of regions governed by warlords, essentially a departure from the nation-state concept where the American-imposed rules-based order provided us with clear political boundaries, crossed only with passports and visas?

The protesters, largely Pashtuns from KP, briefly held protests at D-Chowk square but were dispersed after brutal gunfire from the police and army, resulting in an unknown number of casualties—anywhere between 5 and 50, with dozens killed and scores injured. The red line has been crossed—an army firing on its own civilian population, peacefully marching in protest, is unprecedented. The most recent parallels can be drawn to the Czarist police shooting innocent civilians in Petrograd in 1906 and the Tiananmen Square incident in China in 1989. In the former case, a violent regime change occurred within a decade. In the latter, a brutal dictatorship held firm and made a socio-political contract with the people, though this now shows signs of fraying at the edges.

The recent incidents have shown that any fig leaf of pretence that Pakistan had as a parliamentary democracy has also been done away with. The silence from America is deafening. The US deep state opted for a regime change in Bangladesh with far less provocation. Clearly, Pakistan was always a "very special" client state. Now, the situation has reached a breaking point.

The PTI (representing the will of the common people) has come up against the army (representing the will of the moneyed elites since 1947). Both sides find themselves in an untenable, maximalist position, always an undesirable situation in a limited war. The PTI wants Khan to be released, something the army will never agree to as it would lead to him pushing for fresh elections, galvanising cadres and possibly even becoming the Prime Minister, after which, he may try to cut the army to size (unthinkable for the army). The army finds the status quo favourable as it allows it to continue its hegemony, even if it means that the "country" is reduced to penury and lawlessness.

To a disinterested observer, there does not seem to be a meeting point where both sides can negotiate and compromise to come to an agreeable solution. A former ambassador of Pakistan to the US and the UK, and also the country's permanent representative to the UN, mentioned in a recent podcast that the time for negotiation has passed. What will happen next in this unpredictable chaotic system? The trust of the people in the army was already low, thanks to Khan. However, it is completely shattered and crushed now due to the unprecedented act of the army firing on its own people. For example, past people-led movements in Baluchistan, Sindh and East Pakistan, which were dismissed by the army (and possibly middle-of-the-road Punjabis) as lies and propaganda, also assume salience given the army's recent actions in Islamabad.

The ingredients are ripe for a conflagration, ushering in a chaotic regime with unpredictable outcomes, with the next six months crucial in determining its fate as a post-WW2 nation-state. When the bare minimum position for either side is a maximalist position for the other, it results in a binary view of the world. And in such a view, all bets are off.

Pakistan today satisfies all the scientific conditions for chaotic behaviour. While it is deterministic and not random, it exhibits unpredictable behaviour due to its sensitivity to initial conditions and nonlinearity. These are riveting times for it and its neighbours. Whether borders, de facto or de jure, will undergo revisions in this part of the world is more a question of when than if.

> *When I write here that Pakistan today is still deterministic and not random, I mean that while its condition might be volatile and uncertain, it is not quite ambiguous, to use VUCA terminology.*
>
> *As the world changes from a collection of nation-states to an arrangement of empires, it is more than ever relevant for educated Bhāratiyas to become aware of the fact that we do not fit into the nation-state model, constructed by the West over the last century, to keep its economic interests afloat. This model was literally force fed by the West to an unwilling or unknowing Rest. The new empires of the world, India, China, Russia and USA are seeking their mutual equilibrium. Three of these empires are civilizational, and I for one feel that civilizational states are utterly different from nation-states in terms of their priorities—economic, technological, military and ideological. They need to be governed differently from nation-states and it is for the new intellectual classes of the right wing in Bhārat, in other words, the Hindu Rashtra, to instruct and guide the Rajya in this paradigm.*

End of the Nation State?

CNN News 18, 12 January 2025

Summary: The immediate future portends important and substantive changes for us as the nation-state declines as a platform for the conduct of international relations.

The nation-state, a political entity that is distinguished by uniqueness in language, culture, experience, history and geography, verily most attributes of a people, was birthed in the Thirty Years War and the Treaty of Westphalia in 1648. It is a peculiarly European creation, and came into adolescence with Klemens von Metternich and the 1815 Congress of Vienna. It matured into full adulthood in Versailles at the end of World War I and a welter of new countries started decorating the map of the world, each of them thinking that their political borders were inviolable and forever.

It must not be forgotten that the modern nation-state was forged in the fires of the two world wars; World War II and its end was traumatic for most. After helplessly witnessing Hitler's contempt for the entire nation-state idea, the victors said "Nie wieder" to the concept of changing political borders and under the supervision of the US and the UK came up with a new idea that they called a rules-based order, or in cruder terms, the submission of the entire world to a new world order carefully managed by America to keep its political and economic interests paramount. Permanent borders were a natural corollary, even a condition of the modern nation-state Indeed, apart from a few anomalies, political borders have largely remained fixed in the last 80 years because of the military and economic prowess of the USA, a feature which has been visibly aided by the US dollar's status as the world's reserve currency.

It is sometimes forgotten that in their race to demarcate nation-state borders after 1815 and 1918, the great European powers started cutting up the entire world into entities that 'looked' like nation-states in the sense that they were shown in political maps as 'countries' shaded in bright colours. They did this of course only to advance their economic and geostrategic interests, but reality was far different. These political boundaries outside of Europe were essentially artificial lines drawn on a map and bore no relation to the people they were dividing, their culture, economy, history or background. One merely has to look at the number of straight lines separating these new 'countries' in Africa, West Asia and Central and South America to realize that these boundaries were merely matters of convenience to the European powers that drew them up. Paraguay, Iraq, Nicaragua, Burkina Faso—the list goes on—are 'countries' or shall we say, political constructs that bear no cogent relationship to the people who now inhabit them.

All these lines were not straight. Europeans, more specifically Britishers, were simply fond of drawing lines on maps, straight or crooked. This is their solution to complicated political problems. It just became a habit with them. We have today, the McMahon Line, the Radcliffe Line and the 38th Parallel. These bizarre lines have caused nothing but havoc to the innocent residents of the lands thus vivisected. They even drew a line in the middle of Germany in 1945 and, absurdity of absurdities, Hitler's capital was shared among four countries. Possibly because these latter lines were in Europe, they were reversed in 1989, and while the affected territory might not quite be the Grossdeutschland of 1942, it may still be called Germany.

However, the sanctity of these nation-state boundaries outside of the European heartland may be seriously questioned, for the vast bulk of the Eurasian landmass is civilizational, that is supra-national, and not national. India, China and Russia, the three great civilizational empires of the emerging world, are characterized by geographical regions of 'fuzziness' at their peripheries that buffer their core central areas. These regions include the entire Central Asian region, Pakistan, Afghanistan, Nepal, Bhutan, Bangladesh (or shall we call this East Pakistan?), the two Koreas, the Philippines, Myanmar, Chinese Taipei, Thailand and even Tibet, Sinkiang and Mongolia. Traditionally, before 1945, and certainly before 1914, there were no sharp borders separating most of these areas and people moved and travelled easily enough through them without passports and visas, mostly for economic and commercial purposes—the successors to the old Golden Road and Silk Routes.

However, what would happen if the original guarantor(s) of these nation-state borders themselves decided to break their own rules—again for economic and geostrategic reasons? We do not think that any rational geopolitical observer or average political commentator would have imagined (till very recently) that such a situation could or would ever happen. This is why recent discourse in the US about renewed American territorial expansionism in the manner of Alaska, California and Puerto Rico should not be dismissed as mere filibusters. There might be a tendency to dismiss some of these utterances as delusions of an overenthusiastic far right Republican flank, but it must not be forgotten that a lot of it is being sanctioned by the very top of the Republican establishment which, in a matter of days, will be the new American establishment.

Donald Trump has openly stated his intentions to buy (acquire through other means) Greenland, seize the Panama Canal, absorb

Canada as the 51st state of the USA and rename the Gulf of Mexico. Such a statement has not been made by a US president since the Louisiana purchase in the early days of the Manifest Destiny which resulted in the US nearly doubling its land area. While the action (or inaction) of Trump in this regard will be debated to death by the commentariat in the Amerisphere, its true long term impact may lie elsewhere.

Most of the world outside Europe and America is probably looking for this border freeze to be lifted so that they might redraw their own boundaries, to a greater or lesser extent, in a manner that they feel better suits their natural disposition and character. Several of these rearrangements might even be carried out amicably among the involved parties. Given that it is Asia and Africa that primarily bore the brunt of these artificial lines, the relief in these capitals will be palpable. Indeed, the situation in much of the world between Turkey and the Korean peninsula is metastable with an anticipation as to when the ashes of the current geopolitical order will be immersed in the Ganga, Sindhu, Mekong, Salween and the Euphrates so that more natural topographic and cultural boundaries substitute in its place.

One risk for other nations that might try to start an expansionist spree of their own will be textbook imperial overreach or trying to bite off more than what they can chew. Indeed, if China tries to annex Vietnam or if Russia attempts to dominate Japan it would be nothing short of a disaster. However, past precedence in Asian capitals would show us that this might not happen: foreign policy tends to be more pragmatic. For Bharat, the present time might well be an opportune moment to resurrect Kautiliyan thought and infuse it more deeply into our strategic community and its foreign policy actions, instead of just touting it as a historical muse which might at best win us lukewarm plaudits from here and there.

May we suggest that the reversion of Gilgit-Baltistan and PoJK to Bhārat, with a concomitant splitting off of Balochistan, Sindhudesh and the reassimilation of Khyber Pakhtunkhwa into a greater Afghanistan is now more than a probability? We aver that it has become an immediate possibility. Balochistan and Afghanistan for example may well readjust their present artificial boundary so that Pashtuns are located in just the latter country. Readjustment of the Baloch people in Iran and Balochistan might be more complicated but even here, anything is possible if the rules based order declines in its importance.

Since the political winds are blowing towards civilisation as a truer basis of political identity, such cartographic changes would only reflect the rising aspirations of the vast majority of the world's peoples, whose innermost cravings for a restoration of their genuine, shall we say native or primaeval, identities, have begun to assert themselves because of their rising economic influence. Bharatiyas surely head this list of wronged peoples as we have possibly suffered the worst with the creation of that most artificial of nation-states, Pakistan. The immediate future portends important and substantive changes for us as the nation-state declines as a platform for the conduct of international relations.

> *Balochistan is perhaps an ideal example of a small nation-state that can coexist comfortably at the tri-junction of the three great Eurasian empires of the 21st century.*

Balochistan: An Evolving Geopolitical Transition

Organiser, 10 Apr 2025

Summary: The day-to-day manifestations and their detailed analyses, in terms of troop movements or possible alignments of ethnic groups may be accurate in the immediate temporal context but fail to capture the big picture of the Baloch nation undergoing huge birthing pains as it moves towards a stable political condition as a small country at the periphery of Bhārat, linked to the mother country through economic and cultural ties.

The recent hijacking of the Jaffar Express by insurgents in a remote part of western Pakistan was a watershed moment in a whole sequence of events that have sought secession for the troubled province of Balochistan over the last 80 years. Many defence and security analysts have opined on the history and mechanisms of this insurgency.

Simultaneously, the flare ups in the Pashtun regions of Pakistan are also of note, given the supposed assertions of the security analysts regarding the linking up of the Baloch and Pashtun insurgent groups. In both these peripheral areas of Pakistan, centrifugal forces have been on the rise as this artificial nation-state collapses in front of our eyes.

However, rather than dwell on specific incidents, it might be more worthwhile to analyze them in the context of bigger geopolitical tectonic shifts that have been taking place consequent upon the weakening of the nation-state idea and of the post-WW2 rules-based order with its attendant institutional set-up and organizations. The arrangements whereby the USA has been subsidizing the economies of its vassals and allies have been demolished literally overnight by Donald Trump hastening the demise of the nation-state idea itself. Essentially, the primary architect of this disruption is America seeking to ingest what it created out of the ashes of Mittel Europa like a proverbial Bhasmāsur.

In this context, let us take up the example of Balochistan as a case study. This region might be one of the first to unyoke itself from the burden of the rules-based order, something it has been wanting to do since 1950. Attempting a crystal-ball gaze into the near future one sees how the intermezzo period between the collapse of the post WW2 order on the one hand and a multipolar world on the other might actually play itself out in reality. Specifically, how would naturally organic states like Balochistan, Bhutan or Rakhine morph themselves during the intermediate period between the rules-based order of the past and a future based on multipolarity? How do these evolving nations adjust themselves to the new equilibrium that is now unfolding?

The transition from the Metternich nation state to the post-WW1 dispensation to a stable civilisational state a century later has been and will be a messy affair. In the current interim period, a country like Balochistan spanning two different countries and three different states within Pakistan could well be morphing into a friendly vassal that surrounds the Indian rajya, in the extended domains of Bhāratvarsha. It is noteworthy to point out that what is happening in Balochistan might well have happened in Kurdistan except for the timing; the Kurdish movement peaked at a time when the rules-based order and the nation-state concept were too strong. For Balochistan, the timing is right—the world is ready to see the artificiality of the nation-states that were carved out from the Ottoman Empire after WW1—and recognise the inevitability of a reversal to an older condition where the entire region from the Mediterranean Sea to the Sindhu River consisted of a number of domains separated by soft borders and a free flow of people, trade, commerce and cultural traditions.

Civilizational states are very different from nation states. Bhārat is the dominant civilizational state—one could even call it an empire—in this part of the world. It will have fuzzy borders in the medium term, say by 2035. Balochistan will be one of the nations that buffers the new Bhārat from West Asia and located in one of the fuzzy regions. The Baloch nation today covers all of the Pakistani province of the same name, and also regions of eastern Iran, south western Punjab, southern Khyber Pakhtunkhwa and parts of western Sindh. Hard political boundaries have done little justice to the aspirations of the Baloch people who have felt separated by artificial boundaries that are required in a political model that is far removed from the culture and daily life of essentially migratory communities who travelled for reasons of trade and commerce.

It is pertinent to note the unfortunate history of Balochistan post-1947. The Sultan of Kalat, who was suzerain of this region had no wish to join Pakistan at the time of partition. Balochistan was an independent entity for almost a year after which it was forcibly annexed by Pakistan. The province is sparsely populated but of very large area—it accounts for 44% of Pakistan's land mass. It has, however, only 12-15 million people, just 5-7% of Pakistan's population. Most of it is rugged land and yet it is blessed with an enormous number and variety of mineral wealth that includes copper, gold, silver, coal, iron, chromite, limestone, marble and precious stones like rubies, emeralds, and topaz among others—a veritable treasury.

When stable and ordered domains and structures undergo deep rooted changes to new, very different but also stable and ordered domains and structures, the interfacial periods or phases are characterized by disorder, ambiguity, amorphicity and chaos—whether these changes are physical, political or economic. The more different the initial and final states, the more unpredictable and fluxional the intermediate periods. This is precisely where we see Balochistan today. The Baloch people are dispersed in different countries or provinces within these countries. They aspire to a situation where the Baloch nation is also graced with a political identity as an independent country, which would mostly comprise the present province in Pakistan but could also include some adjoining areas in Iran, Khyber Pakhtunkhwa, Punjab and Sindh.

The day-to-day manifestations of this geopolitical disorder are manifested in the form of armed disturbances, attacks on the Pakistani army, civilian killings, sabotage, and general mayhem. Detailed analyses of these events, in terms of troop movements or possible alignments of ethnic groups may be accurate in the immediate temporal context but fail to capture the big picture of the Baloch nation undergoing huge birthing pains as it moves towards a stable political condition as a small country at the periphery of Bhārat, linked to the mother country through economic and cultural ties, blessed by iconic associations such as Hinglaj Mata, one of our hallowed shakti peethas.

While Balochistan might achieve political independence by reverting to its natural boundaries, a similar harking to its cultural roots might take somewhat longer. Both Khyber Pakhtunkhwa and Balochistan have been largely stripped of their cultural markers and moorings because of the root and stem destruction of the Buddhist and Sanātani culture that used to lie at the intersection of the trade routes between Central Asia, Indian subcontinent, Persia and Western Asia.

There will undoubtedly be a new type of economic order in civilizational states and empires and concomitantly a period of uncertainty and flux in the intermediate period of the transition state between the nation-state of Pakistan and an independent Balochistan. Globalization via trade was the economic bedrock of the rules-based order and the nation-state. However, recent events have shown that even this paradigm is now under threat. What would the enabling condition of sovereignty be, of a new Baloch nation? Sovereignty is determined not by the presence of barbed wires and soldiers guarding borders but the ability to control seigniorage profits as well as enforce the acceptance of one's currency within (and possibly outside) one's borders. This is not a new phenomenon but has been true of human civilization since the republican city states of Bhārat and Greece at least 2500 years ago. However, for intermezzo states like Balochistan with fluid borders, this economic condition may not be easy to achieve given the lack of trust in a new currency by the local population as well as limited confidence of cross border investors for fund raising. In such a scenario, these states might default to using a basket of currencies of trading partners that could also include certain cryptocurrencies (instead of over-dependence on a single currency like the US dollar) to determine the value of the local currency. Natural resources or associated goods and services could guarantee the value of the currency to ensure stability. Balochistan might well be the first example of a new global economic paradigm that unfolds in front of our eyes over the next decade. For in the end, it is economics that directs politics.

> *As Bhārat sees itself as an empire rather than a country, it needs to exert its influence to include the whole region of Bharatavarsha. And who better to tell us how than Kautilya?*
>
> *The reader will note that I have included Europe here as a fifth empire. How precise is my depiction?*

India's Chance at Chanakya Neeti as World's Hegemons Remain Distracted by Tariffs

Swarajya, 16 April 2025

While global empires are busy reorienting amidst tariff wars and political realignments, India finds a golden window to resolve its civilizational dilemmas—invoking Chanakya's wisdom to rise quietly, decisively, and irreversibly.

The assumptions that held the world aloft for 80 years have crumbled—both economically and politically—since Donald Trump's inauguration.

There has been an overload of commentaries on matters that are both volatile and uncertain, to use VUCA language. The USA has identified China as its primary, and possibly only, enemy in a new war for global dominance over the next 25 or more years.

The US President is turning the geopolitical clock backwards to a multipolar age of great powers, a so-called fourth turning, where instead of nation-states, there will now be empires surrounded by vassals. Imposing Pax Americana and the rules-based order is too expensive a proposition for the USA today.

It is fiscally draining to be the world's policeman, and with its known proclivity to oscillate between intervention and isolation—reminiscent of yesteryears' empires such as Hanoverian Britain or

Ming China—the USA has re-entered the latter condition: one in which a 'war economy' paradigm ties together fiscal, monetary, industrial, trade, military, and political policy.

Trump ram-rodded a rustic tariff formula based on trade deficits, not caring for the endless asterisks and hyphens characterising economists' understanding of international trade. The world has entered a stage where no economic model will work until the world resettles to find a new political equilibrium.

China, Trump's bête noire, seems to have been economically, diplomatically, and militarily prepared for the US's gambit. If economics is politics with money, politics is economics with power. In the birthing pains of a new world order, and as complex economic interdependencies fray, a world where several systems are simultaneously running is evolving.

The five modern empires—America, China, Russia, India, and Europe—characterise these systems. They are interacting amongst themselves, with no deep-seated enmities save that between the first two. Typical examples of this are the concurrent viabilities of groupings like the Quad, BRICS, I2U2, and the US-Japan-Australia Trilateral, none of which are in dissonance with the others.

The difference between the old nation-state unipolar or bipolar model (G1, G2) and today's civilizational model is that each of the empires is resigned to the other four exercising their local hegemony in their immediate geographical neighbourhoods.

There could be economic overlap between them—not in the free-flowing patterns of nation-states, but more in the nature of piecemeal arrangements. This is multipolarity. Smaller states will become buffers between empires.

Harking back to Mackinder, the importance of physical geographical proximity as a historical and economic pivot is a reality that all nations, including the USA, now recognize. But perhaps the USA has always known this—the Monroe Doctrine is 200 years old.

Bhārat finds itself in an attractive position amid the USA-China tariff wars as a swing state. Its patient handling of its economic, political, and cultural affairs during the past 11 years of the NDA government now stands it in good stead, as it did during the COVID pandemic and the Ukraine war.

It is the favoured second-best alternative for the four other empires: for the USA it is the ideal counterweight to China; for China it stands for regional stability; for Europe it stands for diversification; and for Russia it stands for trade and commerce.

As the USA and China undergo a politically driven, dishevelled economic decoupling, they are likely to remain preoccupied with their core interests. Peripheral issues in the Indian subcontinent will be a low priority for them unless India is sucked into any of their core interest zones of contestation. This allows Bhārat a golden window to sort out its festering civilizational issues and carry out critical reforms to enhance competitiveness.

Even as the overenthusiastic commentariat exaggerates our importance as vishwagurus, one should remember that our economy is only a fifth of China's and a seventh of the USA's—our importance in the grand scheme of things is small. We are below the radar level of the two hegemons. We should use this invisibility to sort out local problems that do not interest them. As economist Ruchir Sharma said, "the most promising hype for any country is none at all."

Employing the idiom of Chanakya, who typifies surrounding kings as equal, inferior, and superior, India is in the enviable position of having two superior kings (USA, China), two equal kings (Russia, Europe), and many inferior kings, all proximal.

Almost taking a leaf from the Arthasastra, Donald Trump has labelled Bangladesh as Modi's backyard. This is a clear signal that the USA will not excessively interfere in India's unilateral actions within Bhāratvarsha any longer.

As for China, it too realises it has neither the time, reason, nor the capability of inflicting pinpricks on India—whether they be in Chittagong, Skardu, or Ladakh. It has its own problems in Tibet, East Turkestan, and above all, Taiwan, to start causing street riots in Murshidabad or Vaniyambadi, or funding insurgents, electoral and otherwise. All these tamashas are now consigned to history's dustbin.

India must confine itself to actions which lie within our natural abilities, given our culture and traditions—it should not make unqualified economic allies with either the USA or China. If the former, China will start its pinpricks; if the latter, we risk antagonising the most powerful of the empires. Opinions will vary, but a 70% tilt towards the USA, with sufficient economic mollification for the Chinese, seems reasonable. To reiterate, neither of these empires cares about how internal reengineering is undertaken by us—whether it is sama, dana, bheda, or danda.

For India to become Bhārat, we must settle the unresolved issues of Partition, an outrage inflicted on us by the cynical self-aggrandisement of our colonisers in a previous era.

Unless we address and admit that there are 615 million Muslims living in India, Pakistan, and Bangladesh among the 1.1 billion Hindus in India—not to speak of the hapless 25 million in Bangladesh and 4 million in Pakistan—and that the attitudes of a third of those who inhabit Bhāratavarsha are at best equivocal towards the dominant two-thirds majority, we deny ourselves a Hindu Rashtra and Dharmic constitution.

In other words, we deny ourselves the chance to overturn the existing order within our empire and its environs, as Donald Trump is attempting with his American empire.

Civilizational issues are the gap between India and Bhārat, and are also the gap between us and the two hegemons. To lessen the gap, we must hold sway over the extended Bhāratvarsha from Kandahar to Mandalay and from the ocean to the mountains. The innate civilizational unity of Bhārat, cemented by its organic diversity, has been the case for millennia.

The Vishnu Purana makes a pointed reference when it says: "Uttaram yat samudrasya, Himadreshchaiva dakshinam, varsham tad Bharatam nama, Bharati yatra santatihi." The defining feature of Bhāratavarsha is geographical, not creedal.

Undoubtedly, India has made many preparations to smoothen things out in this regard in our neighbourhood, with respect to domains in Nepal, Bhutan, Myanmar, Gilgit-Baltistan, Balochistan, Sindh, Afghanistan, and Khyber Pakhtunkhwa.

These arrangements were made largely during the previous world order (pre-Trump), and of necessity were circumspect and discreet. A wise country would follow Deng Xiaoping's advice to hide one's strength and bide one's time. But the time to show one's strength has come, and we can finally afford to punch above our weight—in the confidence of America's shrewd blessing.

The natural question that arises in the minds of many Bhāratiyas is: which of our self-avowed Islamic protuberances should warrant immediate attention? Chanakya again provides an answer when he asks which is to be marched against—an assailable enemy involved in troubles to a greater degree or a strong enemy troubled to a lesser degree?

Let us assume that Bangladesh is the assailable enemy while Pakistan is the strong enemy. Chanakya is clear in his answer and says that the conqueror should march against the strong enemy under less troubles first, for the troubles of the strong enemy, though less, will multiply when attacked.

Clearly, this will come true—even small pinpricks we deliver now in Pakistan can result in an amplified domino collapse, and Gilgit-Baltistan can simply deliver itself into the Union of India, where it always legally belonged, without a shot being fired from our side. We would be only following the other great Asian war exponent, Sun Tzu, who advocated victory in war without fighting.

After this, the existence of Pakistan itself will come into question, and the other empires will be ready to cut their own deals with India, which would have finally recovered its access to Central Asia.

To conclude, Chanakya describes the king as one who is possessed of foresight, ready to avail of opportunities when afforded in respect of place, time, and manly efforts, clever enough to discern the causes necessitating the cessation of treaty or war with an enemy, to avail himself of the enemy's weak points—and all this with no loss of dignity or secrecy.

The king of today's India will assure for himself a place in history if he seizes the moment. To use the cliché: timing isn't the main thing—it is the only thing.

> *And now we come to the non-linear kinetic moment in our relationship with Pakistan. Or is it not even a relationship any more, and merely a situation?*

Operation Sindoor Is Just the Beginning

Swarajya, 7 May 2025

Summary: The present situation with regard to Sindoor and Pakistan is a case of history taking a turn in front of our eyes.

The much anticipated reprisal against Pakistan has finally come with a strategic pinpointed assault on terrorist camps and hideouts in Bahawalpur, Muzaffarabad, Muridke and other locations in Pakistani Punjab and Pakistan-occupied Jammu & Kashmir.

The attacks were carefully calibrated and well thought out by targeting only terrorist facilities, avoiding military and civilian targets—for the time being. The government of India has shown admirable strategic thinking in several senses.

Firstly, the indiscriminate shelling across the LoC within an hour of our attack on Bahawalpur is a tacit admission by the authorities in Pakistan that they have been harbouring terrorists all along. This came days after Pakistan's Defence Minister said that terrorism was merely "dirty work for the West".

Let it not be forgotten that after Balakot, Pakistan denied that it even happened. However, the magnitude and intensity of our present assault has forced them to admit that terror, the Pakistani State, and the Pakistani army are essentially synonymous and co-instrumentalities.

The sophistication of the attack, the events leading up to it, and especially statements made by leaders of other major countries and the statements of our own leaders, leave no doubt that there was excellent teamwork and coordination in the various wings of our government throughout the previous two weeks. It is not difficult to join the dots. Statements made by the US President and Vice President as well as the US Secretary of State, leave no doubt that the US had no objection and possibly even encouraged India to destroy the terror camps. At the same time, both the USA and India had probably agreed that escalation into an outright military conflict between the two countries was definitely undesirable in the early stages of the wider undertaking to dismantle Pakistan.

A strategic phone call from the Russian President two days before Operation Sindoor was another indication that the pincers were closing in on Pakistan. No less significant is the clinching of the Indo-UK trade deal again just a couple of days ago, a deal that has moved at a turtle's pace for many years, and which was probably clinched with India extracting a very heavy price from the UK in terms of it at least temporarily abandoning its pro-Pakistani tilt in the conflict. The UK needs India too badly economically to wade into India-Pakistan matters right now. The lack of any weighty comment from China after Sindoor also indicates its guarded stance towards the whole matter, for in the end, if the State of Pakistan ceases to exist, China's adversarial position against India would be downright disadvantageous.

Sindoor is just the beginning. The attack has been cleverly planned so that Pakistan loses whether it carries out a retaliatory strike beyond the LoC or whether it does nothing in response to our attack. Let us consider these two possibilities. The USA is probably pressuring Pakistan at this point in time not to escalate the matter militarily, because if that were to happen, it knows that it cannot prevent India from carrying out a disproportionate kinetic response. The canard of two nuclear powers engaged in a military conflict does not have any serious takers. India will not use the nuclear option first, and Pakistan knows it cannot use the nuclear option because if it did, it would cease to exist.

Pakistan is essentially caught in a bind. If it provides a big kinetic retort, the overwhelming Indian counter-response will cause it to lose large amounts of territory with inevitable centrifugal consequences among its provinces. If it does nothing, the army which is the power centre in Pakistan will lose considerable face among the Pakistani people and will be unable to retain power. In earlier times, calls for Ghazwa-e-Hind or Kashmir banega Pakistan were more than enough for the people to retain confidence in their army. Today even the virulent hatred that Pakistanis have for India in general and Hindus in particular will not be enough for them to maintain any kind of advantage in the ongoing conflict. Psychological deterioration will set in relatively quickly in that country, and all psychological defeats are defeats until death—1971 is a good enough example.

India is mounting a multi-directional attack on our enemy, and now there is little doubt that the aim of the Modi Government is the complete dismemberment of the Pakistani State and a full resolution of all partition related issues, an injustice that was done to Bharat by the Anglo-American cabal at the time of independence. India is sufficiently strong economically, and the USA, Russia, and China, the three other empires of the modern world, are all weaker in relative terms than they were 10 years ago. India has correctly recognised the golden window of opportunity in seeking the complete removal of the Pakistani State. The water wars from the north and control of Gwadar and Karachi from the south are undoubtedly a part of the master plan over the next 2-3 years.

Pakistan was created to suit the interests of Britain and America, but today it suits the interests of neither America, Russia, or even China to exist in its present form. All these other empires would prefer to deal with a strong India and a gaggle of smaller States like Sindhudesh, Balochistan and Pashtunistan. A Punjabistan rump could always be maintained as an insurance policy by the Americans in case India becomes too strong or powerful by 2035. In the short run, the US seems to be assisting India as it engages in sabre-rattling with China. In the medium run, it would not like India to become another China. In the end, America would become extremely nervous if Bharat, Russia, and China were to form a united Eurasian conglomerate 15 years from now.

All in all, the present situation is a case of history taking a turn in front of our eyes, and it would certainly become a textbook example of how geopolitics is conducted between empires in the 21st century.

"Will you not stop quoting laws to us who are girded with swords?" – Life of Pompey, Plutarch

Sindoor goes on. It did not stop on 10 May 2025. The hinge to our aims to dismember Pakistan is, to my mind, Gilgit-Baltistan.

Even after Operation Sindoor, Gilgit-Baltistan Will Be Crucial to the Bigger Picture

CNN News 18, 8 May 2025

Summary: The reclamation of Gilgit-Baltistan will be a strategic and economic watershed moment for Bhārat.

Operation Sindoor has electrified the nation, sorrowing and grieving after the dastardly terrorist attack in Pahalgam on 22 April. The nation's resolve has been made a reality by the Modi government in the form of decisive action against the perpetrators of terror and their supporters with attacks on Bahawalpur, Muridke and Muzaffarabad among others. Twenty-four hours later, it is now amplified into a systematic attack on the air defence systems in the largest and most strategically vital cities of Pakistan—Lahore, Karachi, Sialkot, Peshawar, Astore, and even Rawalpindi. The defence minister has more than delivered what he promised, in that the people of India got what they wanted. They will probably get even more.

Exceeding mere revenge or revanchism, however, public sentiment has transcended emotionality, and is seeking a long-term solution to the blight known as Pakistan, and settle forever the unresolved issues of partition. How our country and its armed forces achieve this goal, in what timeframe, and by employing which means is not the subject of this piece. In fact, this would be a futile exercise in a war situation where events are changing by the hour. Instead, we attempt to understand why the return of Gilgit-Baltistan to Bharat is of paramount importance.

Before advancing further, it is important to understand what Pakistan is and why it exists. These questions are strongly interrelated. In essence, Pakistan is a geography for hire under an extractive elite, eager to find a larger power to which it may sell its geography. Pakistan, in essence, is the Sindhi and Baloch coastline on one end, the gates to Central Asia on the other (via Khyber Pakhtunkhwa onto Tajikistan and Afghanistan), with a Muhajir-Punjabi elite enriching themselves off the connection between these two ends and the intervening land. This elite called upon the British, the Americans, the Gulf States, and then finally the Chinese to successively rent out Pakistan's geography, which connects the western Indian Ocean to the Central Asian heartland and beyond, and incidentally fund their debauchery in upscale neighbourhoods in Islamabad and Lahore.

The government is the Pakistani State but the power lies with the army. Pakistan's bloated and ruthless army is the obvious conduit for this business of geographic renting and feudal landlordism because controlling (and immiserating) disparate ethnicities with their own sense of history, and preventing a population reduced to serfdom from demanding economic betterment, requires extensive use of force. The bogeyman of India, or the rabble-rousing calls of Ghazwa-i-Hind, were convenient distractions to paper over the severe internal contradictions existing within Pakistan.

The above scheme was not an accident, or a case of convoluted historical evolution, but of conscious design. Pakistan's history can be reduced to transactions between roughly 70 families, many of who were zamindars wary of pre-independence socialists who intended to place land ceilings and found a convenient way of retaining holdings by demanding a separate State altogether, control all institutions (including the military and judiciary) within and beyond the Pakistani State.

This elite inspired great confidence in the British, such that they could set up a suitable entity providing sufficient leverage in the region. Thus, Cyril Radcliffe carved out a geographical oddity which connected the heartland with the rimland, and could be intermeshed with the British coastal colonies such as Aden and Singapore, perched upon global sea lanes of communication. Unsurprisingly, Karachi port remained directly in British hands till 1979, and indirectly thereafter.

While the plan was in motion by 1947, one major complication remained. Even though the Pakistani coast was secured, Jammu & Kashmir held out from joining Pakistan. The reason was obvious—Jammu, Kashmir, Gilgit, Kargil-Baltistan, and Ladakh are separate geographies, separate peoples, and have separate religious beliefs. However, this rendered the creation known as Pakistan with severely limited utility, since access to Central Asia remained cut off. Central Asia, at the time, was the setting for a second round of the Great Game, where Soviet writ held sway.

A physical land border of the sympathetic Soviets with a socialist India might have spelled disaster for the West at large, since they were already seeing that Soviet assistance to communist forces in the then-raging Chinese Civil War was turning the tide in favour of the reds. A strong India could frustrate Western planning of keeping the country under soft colonisation, and India's location could sever the West from access to Asia by sea altogether. Further, parts of Gilgit-Baltistan showed evidence that uranium may be lying there—a critical material for nuclear weapons, of which Britain did not have any natural reserves. These factors made Jammu and Kashmir, especially Gilgit-Baltistan, indispensable to British plans in the 1940s.

Thus, one of the worst cases of post-colonial treachery was executed in 1947. At the time, the Indian and Pakistani armies were still manned by British officers. Large parts of today's Gilgit, at the time, were under British administration, under a structure known as the Gilgit Agency, whereby the British Empire had forced the Maharajas to hand over large tracts which abutted Central Asia and Afghanistan. Major William Brown, a British officer, was manning a unit of the Maharaja's troops in the Gilgit Agency known as the Gilgit Scouts.

In October 1947, Major Brown mutinied unopposed against his own army, took over Gilgit, linked up with Pakistani marauders who had begun a campaign of ethnic cleansing against Hindus, and held a sham referendum where the people of Gilgit supposedly demanded accession to Pakistan. His mutiny was rewarded by the British government with an award of the Order of the British Empire (an award of great esteem) in 1948, and his continued stay in Pakistan till 1959. As is obvious, the British had arranged for the whole affair, and had successfully secured a valuable crossroads in the form of Gilgit-Baltistan between India, Central Asia, and the Indian Ocean via Karachi. Unsurprisingly, Chinese interests are concentrated in Gilgit-Baltistan as well.

The erasure of the stain of the continued occupation on what is legally Indian land naturally evokes much pain in us. Even if we choose to stick to the outcome of the foolish decision to take the invasion to the UN, the legal sleight of hand played by Pakistan in making the world, even Indians, forget that the very first operative condition of the UN resolution on the matter is a complete and unconditional Pakistani withdrawal is a great diplomatic failure on our part. How much of this inability was due to foreign powers exerting pressure remains unknown. From Baltistan to Chitral, and from Poonch to Shaksgam, an incontrovertible legal claim was relegated to just ink on paper, with even reclamations made during the 1971 war abandoned when foreign powers' access to Central Asia via Gilgit-Baltistan was threatened.

However, much water has flown under the bridge since. The withdrawal of the USA from Afghanistan marks a watershed moment, where faraway powers are downsizing their presence in the heartland, and concentrating on the rimland instead. India has shed its socialistic infatuations, and has become a power to reckon with. With India willing to trade freely, and even offer limited military access through landmark agreements like the LEMOA with the USA, the logic with which Pakistan was established has ceased to exist. The fact of the matter is that the business model underpinning Pakistan finds no takers today, and has become obsolete.

A scramble for Pakistan is well underway between global powers, USA, China, India and Russia, and maybe even settled amongst them. Large tracts of Khyber Pakhtunkhwa have fallen to the Afghans and their proxies, while Balochistan's independence movement cannot be ignored anymore. Sindh too has some interesting murmurs. Occupied Jammu & Kashmir and occupied Ladakh (containing Gilgit-Baltistan) are already gravely restive. Global powers find it in their interest to see an independent Balochistan which can be dealt with directly, or an independent Sindh which exists as a Belgium-like buffer entity for the rest of the world to trade through.

The rump of Pakistani Punjab, which dominates Pakistan's affairs, is a severe inconvenience for all involved. It makes much more sense for global powers to cooperate with India, and with individual provinces of interest, instead of the artificial creation known as Pakistan. It is thus not surprising that Chinese help has become severely limited, with talks of 'taller than the Himalayas' and 'sweeter than honey' replaced with increasingly harsh loan conditions and anger on destroyed military equipment tanking the marketability of Chinese equipment worldwide. The USA has all but become hostile too, with a supposed endorsement of secessionist movements.

It is portentous that Russia maintains a distance, perhaps anticipating access to warm water ports via a Bharat that has reclaimed Gilgit-Baltistan. The Gulf, eager to distance itself from radical Islam and to embrace trade, finds much to gain if Pakistan were to cease to exist in its present form. Pakistan was born to serve the interests of others; now, there is no one interested in the entity's continued existence.

Hence, the timing of events in which we find ourselves presents a historical opportunity to begin the process of finally resolving the tragedies and unresolved questions of the partition. The time for action is thus nigh upon us. Military action and legal or civilisational claims aside, the end of the story should rightfully be from where it began, i.e., Gilgit-Baltistan. While sabre-rattling plays out across occupied territory, the pressure on Gilgit-Baltistan is the most crippling for Pakistan.

The return of Gilgit-Baltistan will cause a massive shift in the strategic thinking, reach, and power projection of Bharat. Bharat will, after almost a gap of a century, become a key player in Central Asia, and offer itself as a much-needed strategic alternative to China in the region. This will also enable Central Asia as well as Russia to find access to the Indian Ocean, and for India to get access to the Arctic.

Gilgit-Baltistan will extend Bharat's strategic presence to hitherto untouched areas, and trigger a strong rethink amongst Russia and China to imagine a truly Eurasian future, where none can afford to ignore Bharat.

Gilgit-Baltistan's economic potential could also lead to new avenues of economic growth. It has historically been an entrepot between Afghanistan, China, Bharat, the Russian far East, and Tibet; a reactivation of the region's silk-trade era prowess will rearrange domestic and global supply chains. This region is also crucial to Bharat to secure critical minerals and energy from Central Asia and Russia, apart from reactivating and rejoining silk-road era trade routes. With Sagarmala along the coasts, a Girimala along the Himalayas with Gilgit-Baltistan as its fulcrum holds potential to supercharge Indian economic growth and supply chain power. This will make Bharat the primus inter pares in a transcontinental trading bloc, which will inevitably also lead to the export of Bharatiya trade and digital public infrastructure.

The reclamation of Gilgit-Baltistan will be a strategic and economic watershed moment for Bharat, and coupled with the strong legal basis for the same, the region remains the prime contender for its ghar waapasi. However, the civilizational confidence such a move will instill in India, and the demoralisation it will inflict on the Ghazwa-i-Hind extremists, will lead to a resolution of many problems in the subcontinent and the country. Unsurprisingly, while missiles rained over Pakistani military installations, a hue and cry emerged from rioters in Darbhanga, peddlers of fake news eager to demoralise the nation presiding over newspapers and TV studios, and so-called pacifists in upmarket neighbourhoods across the country—Lutyens, South Mumbai, Park Street and Cathedral Road.

The problem of Pakistan is only a facet of a broader issue of the coalition which wishes to destroy Bharat and Bharatiyata, and is often labelled the Mullah-Missionary-Marxist axis. The fall of Pakistan will, thus, pulverise enemies within and without, and lead to an all-out efflorescence in Bharat. The Bharatiya civilisational revival will stand vindicated and reinvigorated with the recovery of some of its Bhumi, and while Westphalian norms will receive a final burial, the march towards a truly Bharatiya system of governance will start taking concrete shape. Meanwhile, other regions and peoples may see reason and engage with Bharat. In such a context, Gilgit-Baltistan's unique history and potential accord it a special long-term significance.

Events over the past few days indicate that the return of Gilgit-Baltistan to Bharat may be sooner than what any of us might have imagined; from thinking in terms of years, it may be more realistic to think in terms of months or even weeks, that too without our armed forces firing too many shots. In geopolitical matters, actual events are governed by the dynamics of circumstance rather than the statics of diplomatic exchanges. Many a great country has come and gone throughout history; Pakistan, being just a clumsy arrangement to continue a neocolonial project, may not even warrant a footnote in the years to come.

> *And how does Bhārat operationally go about remaking Pakistan in its scheme for Bhāratavarsha? There can be no compromise on this. Pakistan, in its present form and shape, must go.*

Operation Sindoor and After: Why War of Attrition Must Be Avoided

CNN News 18, 25 June 2025

Summary: Something fundamental seems to have crystallised in India's geopolitical thinking vis-à-vis our strategic perspective on Pakistan.

Scarcely had the embers of Operation Sindoor mellowed, did the world wake up to the eruption of Operation Rising Lion in the Israel–Iran conflict. Even as both operations continue, the world's geopolitical calculus is metamorphosing into a menacing form characterised by VUCA (volatility, uncertainty, complexity, and ambiguity). Even as militaries mobilise, economic and informational warfare are well underway—China's latest restrictions on rare earth magnet exports threaten to bring the mammoth Indian automotive industry to a grinding halt. Salvos are fired not only from missile silos, but through supply chains as well.

In this threnody of war, something fundamental seems to have crystallised in India's geopolitical thinking vis-à-vis our strategic perspective on Pakistan. For the first time ever, we appear to have correctly contextualised that Pakistan's ideological basis of waging war against Bhārat and Hindus aligns fully with the economic and political interests of its army, and that the same cannot be corrected by us through constructive engagement. Secondly, our government has realised that our internal and external enemies form a single continuum—one cannot be treated as separate from the other. Hence, illegals being deported, rioters' houses being bulldozed, and armed attack, all deal with what is essentially the same issue.

Previously, our strategic outlook was to achieve a reorientation in Pakistan, such that it ceases the operations of its terror industry. This was attempted first through détente (social courtesies with Nawaz Sharif), then with disengagement (terror and talks do not go together), and finally by taking punitive action (Balakot). Despite all this, it was impossible to make Pakistan stop using terror as state policy simply because far too many interests depended on its continued intransigence to serve multifarious purposes.

With this certainty, we seem to have finally accepted that only dismantling the State of Pakistan can guarantee India's long-term safety and security. So, focus has shifted to degrading Pakistani capabilities (targeting its air defense) and striking at its very viability (reducing downstream flows from the Indus system; banning trade via third countries). Our objective, simply stated, would be to balkanize Pakistan. The baffled reactions from some sections of our noisy commentariat seem to indicate that our government's decisive change in orientation is indeed on the right lines.

The ongoing conflict in Iran will undoubtedly have Pakistan being used by both sides of the conflict at times, depending on whose bid is higher. However, unlike the Afghan conflict in the past, Pakistan is today not indispensable either to the USA or to China. It is hence prone to being punished by either of these major powers if it tries to play one against the other. In all likelihood, it will end up with burnt fingers, or be taken for granted as a helpless vassal. The era of limitless foreign help propping up Pakistan for it to pretend that it has any semblance of parity with us is over.

In such circumstances, India's path ahead will be challenging, with every assault against Pakistan met with domestic disturbances and feigned international consternation. However, there is no turning back for us. India must fight, and alone, as all its enemies reveal themselves as a single entity.

The critical element in fulfilling India's objectives concerning Pakistan will be to prevent its local conflict from being turned into a theater for a broader global war. Both sides, Western as well as Chinese, would be greatly interested in pulling Bhārat down into a longer, messier conflict as in the Ukraine, destabilising its hard-earned political stability and derailing its economic rise. If anything, a singular, long conflict with Pakistan will greatly delay our $5+ trillion GDP ambitions. Such a delay may prove unaffordable for us, since all of our projections hinge upon making a transition to an economic power of a magnitude that we cannot be ignored or defeated by others, but only dealt with by them.

In summary, the twin national security imperatives of dismantling the State of Pakistan, and becoming a $5+ trillion (ultimately, $10+ trillion) economy need to be addressed simultaneously. To us, it seems there is only one credible strategy to attain our economic ambitions and that is to fuse sustained non-kinetic means of degrading Pakistan's capabilities (water, trade, etc.) with intense short kinetic actions, such as the first phase of Operation Sindoor, so that we take out critical assets and military capabilities of the enemy. A war of attrition is to be avoided at all costs.

The distinction between the civilian and the military in Pakistan will have to be discarded once and for all; a nation as radicalised as Pakistan is no less a threat than their terrorist army, they are for all intents and purposes, part of a singular whole. The civilian in Pakistan becomes a conduit to portray victimhood, and a tool to manufacture instability. In turn, let us also be realistic about those who may be citizens of India on paper, but are animated by foreign intrigues in their hearts and maybe wallets.

We must secure the western and northwestern frontiers of the subcontinent. History stands testament to the fact that it is in these areas where our geographical vulnerabilities have been most fully exposed over centuries. As West Asia destabilises, the threat of terrorists from West Asia landing up here is a real one as long as Pakistan continues to facilitate the same. To set up Balochis and Pashtuns as the first line of defense for a shared subcontinental future, beginning with the military but ultimately culminating in the civilizational through economics, should be a medium-term goal for Bhārat.

However, more immediately, what may we expect given our government's recent actions? With water volumes down all across Pakistan, their kharif crop will be poor. The pressure on the army to keep peddling higher doses of anti-Hindu jingoism will be high. Our immediate neighbourhood will continue to fester, mostly through foreign insistence. Misinformation will be peddled by the foreign-funded ecosystem pervading the media and our politics. We need to be watchful, and stay steadfast. Post-monsoons, Pakistan may face floods via the Indus with our blessings; things may take a particularly ugly turn militarily as the first snows begin blocking passes in the Himalayas and the Hindu Kush, even as another window of opportunity opens for Bhārat. Winters have helped or harmed armies on more than one occasion in world history, and we project that a winter war can decisively favour us in 2025.

The world will be frigid towards the security of our country, with perhaps the exception of a few countries like Israel, which face a similar predicament. The closer we move towards winter, temperatures in and around Bhārat are expected to soar. Our future will be forged in the fires we are still to face; we cannot continue to let down our future generations with inaction clothed as conscientiousness.

"The era of procrastination, of half-measures, of soothing and baffling expedients, of delays is coming to its close. In its place we are entering a period of consequences." — Winston S. Churchill in 1936 on the eve of World War II.

This was my most recent take on Pakistan. It needs to be wiped off the face of the map and split into four or five countries if Bhārat is to survive. The quotation of Churchill is one of my all time favourites. It says so much about how India has been run in the last 80 odd years.

Sindoor continued to occupy my thoughts. Why is the final solution of the Pakistan problem so important for Bhārat? I was thinking a lot about war itself, possibly in anticipation of my forthcoming book "India's Supply Chains in a World at War", which will probably appear just before this book that you are reading now.

A Nation at War: OpSindoor Continues

CNN News 18, 20 August 2025

The terms 'war' and 'peace' are often defined imprecisely in world history. Is peace merely defined by the absence of mobilised militaries engaging in pitched battles? Clearly not – war is taken as any adversarial interaction in which rivals compete, using all methods, be they military or otherwise, to subdue the other party. By this token, India and Pakistan have been at war for exactly 78 years, even as I write this on Independence Day 2025 as a gedanken experiment.

The orthodox Clausewitzian definition of war as nothing other than a continuation of policy by other means, is sufficient to convey to us how governments use war, even if it does not define accurately what war is in itself. In any event, all wars are derived from state policy and lead almost directly to strategic concerns. Strategy may be defined as the use of battles to win the war. Strategy is future oriented: it is a declaration of intent by a government and an indicator of the possible means required to fulfil that intent. Strategy combines means, ways and ends. It is designed to make war usable by the state so that it may fulfil its political objective.

In the India-Pakistan context our overall policy would be the contain Pakistan so that it does not pose a physical danger to us, sharing as it does a long land boundary across flat plains and deserts. Another policy aim would be to restrain the country from exploiting religious differences within India considering that more Muslims live in India than in Pakistan, their ancestors having opted to remain in the mother country even in the backdrop of a religion-based partition. Finally, there is the long-term goal of undoing some of the mistakes of partition, the so-called unfinished agenda; for example, could OpSindoor progress to OpSindhu? Whether any or all of these policy aims are resolved now, later or never is not known to any of us. However, they are the guiding principles of any war that has been fought with Pakistan in the past, is being fought at the present or will be fought in the future.

Our strategic thinking vis-à-vis Pakistan has been concerned with maintaining our relationships with other countries, notably the USA, China and Russia, and to a smaller extent Europe and the Gulf states so that we maintain some degree of say, economic relationship with these countries that they would be averse to disturb in the event of an all-out conflict with Pakistan. For example, our oil trade with Russia was not disturbed by OpSindoor because of our excellent relations with Russia. Another strategic concern would be to decide whether, in the case of a military movement to take territory, a strike on Gilgit-Baltistan or PoJK, across the LoC, would be preferable compared to a strike on Punjab or Sind across the IB, from purely political considerations. Along these lines, a further strategic consideration would be to evaluate if a carrying forward of the war through a friendly Baluchistan or KP would be better than a direct assault on Pakistan across the LoC or IB.

From policy to strategy one moves to tactics employed in the field of war, however one defines it, in the physical space, the cyber space or the cognitive space. Tactics are operational aspects of a war that take into account the ever-changing nature of the battlefield, the enemy, the circumstances, the unexpected and the all-important time factor that might change any of these above-mentioned factors at relatively short notice. In the Pakistan context, tactics would consist of questions such as whether one should attack in October or November this year, how one should use drones, whether there should be feint dummy attacks in distant places before the real thing, or even whether an attack across the LoC would be preferable to one across the IB, but now from purely tactical considerations, not political ones.

One therefore constructs a troika view of war as a logical sequence of policy, strategy and tactics with some intersection of these three domains. Policy, at least in a democracy like India, is ultimately determined by the people through elections, and is often a matter of emotion. Strategy is the responsibility of the government and is cerebral in its basis, following from confidential discussions and internal deliberations. Tactics are almost always best left to the military establishment; it has been a pity that in the past, the civilian governments have interfered with tactical questions, keeping their political priorities in mind. It has been a refreshing change that in OpSindoor, there has been no interference in the tactical pursuit of the war against Pakistan in all the above-mentioned war spaces: physical, cognitive and cyber. Tactics are neither emotional nor cerebral – they are mostly mathematical, operational and time dependent.

Let us now look at OpSindoor so far in the context of the other 1½ enemies faced by India. In the context of China, one would have to think about whether or not, in the event of a major escalation of hostilities, it would provide boots-on-the-ground support to Pakistan, create disturbances in the India-China border or content itself with growls in the UN and other forums.

As for the half-enemy faced by us internally, it is a matter of regret that this ½-enemy has, for reasons both political and economic, been actively working to unseat a lawfully elected government, and sadly enough even if it means it compromises the unity and integrity of the country and possibly even its disintegration and dismemberment, by consorting with unfriendly foreign powers recklessly and wantonly. This is another war we need to fight and not necessarily militarily; the people of this country need to fight an all-out war against our internal enemies in non-kinetic ways. Further extensions of OpSindoor will almost be extended from being purely military operations to other forms of warfare with the overall aim of vanquishing the enemy.

The government – and most recently the Chief of Army Staff – have explicitly stated that OpSindoor is still going on – what was decided on 10 May was merely a cessation of hostilities. Some water has flown below the bridge since then with POTUS Trump's tantrums, his tilt towards Pakistan and our PM's discussions with President Putin and the announcement of his forthcoming visit to China in early September. The COAS has stated in public that he expects a further round of hostilities soon and that third countries might actively intervene in support of Pakistan. The CDA chief has in the meantime stated that wars start in today's world even without formal declarations.

What is new in the 'new normal' created in OpSindoor is that India can wage war against Pakistan in the new technological era, and that might not hesitate to escalate the war at a time of its choosing. By threatening the fading rules-based order of the USA, India has shown that it might have the necessary chutzpah to punch slightly above its weight in OpSindoor Phase II. The USA cannot be unconcerned as it sees in India's moves and actions, a repeat of China's actions 15 to 20 years ago. The spectre of two large Asian civilisational states that are economically and militarily powerful by 2040 would well signal the end of the USA as primus inter pares in the international high table of nations.

The mood of the Indian public is unambiguous – they consider the currency of victory in war as enemy territory - and only this. Nothing else will suffice for them. Two possibilities suggest themselves: the first is the seizure of a part or the whole of the territory that India has always considered as hers – by legal considerations. I refer, of course, to the districts of Gilgit, Baltistan and PoJK, namely the areas between Muzaffarabad, Poonch and Mirpur. Taking these areas would involve crossing the LoC which, legally speaking, will not cause excessive consternation in the international community, barring possibly China. The second possibility would involve crossing the IB at unspecified points and taking territory. This second possibility flies in the face of the so-called rules-based order and inviolability of the post-1945 nation-state boundaries. However, these boundaries have been crossed recently in Ukraine and a while ago in the Horn of Africa and are by no means sacrosanct, their 'inviolability' only depending on the power of the US hegemon in world affairs. This latter power diminishing latterly, such borders will be crossed with increasing impunity.

In such a scenario, Pakistan remains the final block in our smooth passage towards becoming an international power of the first order. This is probably the reason the Indian State is considering a continuation of OpSindoor towards achieving this most prized currency of victory of war against Pakistan - land.

Now a little bit more about war and warriors—but of a different type.

Indian Entrepreneurship in Times of War

CNN News 18, 11 June 2025

India has got habituated to a hard wiring of its intellectual capabilities, after six decades of losing a substantial number of its engineers and technically qualified personnel to the USA or to stultifying employment in Indian megacities where they burn out in a couple of decades. Even today, the sons and daughters of well-heeled businessmen do not wish to augment the value that only they can bring to their family company but rather prefer to sell their talent at a CTC that is a fraction of their intrinsic value to their lucky employer.

It is understood at top levels that foundational change is required across all institutions that have acted subservient to prolonged colonial interests to the extent that our young minds feel more aligned to external interests rather than feeling that they need to be a part of the economic revival of Bhārat.

What is entrepreneurship? It is the transition of an activity that starts with an individual and goes on to become an organisation with a financial outcome. For a nation with ambitions suppressed for decades, and the largest young population, we have dreams waiting to be realised. Entrepreneurship steers one away from seeking set patterns of talent for sale that employment represents towards an expanding ecosystem where an entire supply chain of individuals steers towards disproportionate financial rewards.

What is war? Taking a disinterested view of things, humankind is living in one of the apparently most 'peaceful' eras it has ever known. Armed strife remains localized, and transcontinental devastation wrought by the ravages of war have been relegated to faint memories. Yet, is peace defined merely by the absence of mobilized militaries engaging in pitched battles? Or can the supposed converse of peace, namely war, be taken as any adversarial interaction in which rivals compete using any and all methods whatsoever, be they military or otherwise? Wars today are economic, social, cultural and ideological, and may even be waged using food and yes, even water as weapons.

War is everywhere. It is a system of rewards and consequences for winners and losers. It is not very different from the jungle world of predators and prey. Corporate wars that eat local businesses and pharma wars that threaten millions with manipulating health diagnostics are today's wars. Like all wars they are unacceptable because in one way or the other they threaten the harmony of daily life.

International relations today have become fraught, fickle, transactional and transient as the world discards the so-called rules-based-order and moves towards a no-rules-whatsoever-disorder. The global situation today is truly dynamic. This generalized anarchy has immense consequences for India's economy—especially its entrepreneurial class and the way in which MSMEs need to be restructured in our country.

What are the entrepreneurial changes specifically needed in India in times of war? MSMEs in times of peace are engineered to be in a condition of equilibrium. In times of war, they enter a phase of metastable equilibrium and at the worst, violent disequilibrium leading to their quick collapse. This basic fact needs to be taken into account by young entrepreneurs and venture capital financiers. Here, we highlight two specific aspects that connect MSMEs in a war-like condition that affects the world in general, and India in particular.

The first point we mention is how an MSME should adapt itself to a new way of thinking, whatever be the commodity or service with which it is connected. The second point is how an MSME can connect itself with an activity related to the actual physical and mental war we are engaged in with our two and a half enemies.

Firstly, there is the matter of timing. There are no war whistles. Escalations are quick and unannounced; in a matter of minutes, a drone swarm can appear carrying an arsenal. Preparedness for war in a highly technological environment is being in a state of round the clock readiness. One cannot lapse into complacency at any time. For any sort of MSME, an ability to react quickly to any adverse condition is a must. For this, back up plans are essential and continuous vigilance.

Our current war with Pakistan and with nations dictating new tariffs and sanctions at the drop of a hat we must eschew the compartmentalised approach of industry with its great dependence on foreign Original Equipment Manufactures (OEMs). Just recently with China stopping its export of high flux permanent magnets to India (and also the USA) we seem to have woken up to the fact that China has a virtual monopoly of neodymium supply chains; for neodymium is a rare earth element (REE) that is essential to fabricate these magnets. Why were we sleeping all these days? What we needed was an MSME that might have been geared to finding neodymium deposits in India. Things like this needed to be looked into; instead we encouraged MSMEs that were looking at ice cream that doesn't melt or kirana shops on two wheelers.

An empowered, regional MSME working in closer collaboration with a technological institute (IIT) is a more dependable ally in today's time, as we move to modular engineering. Dual Use Technologies to Interdisciplinary excellence have led to a newer array of mechanisms capable of weaponizing our industrial production on the one hand, and to jeopardising essential services and command centres of the enemy on the other hand. Drones can carry payloads without risking human lives in critical missions at a fraction of the cost of more conventional technologies and without the use of expensive satellites (for surveillance). We need to gear many more MSMEs to drone technology so that we compete effectively with Turkey, Iran and China in this domain. Other technologies like 3D printing, Digital Twins and AI should also find their place in the Indian MSME ecosystem.

What about adaptability? Why should Indian VCs invest in Defence Tech? India's defence budget has been amongst its top three spends running into several hundred thousand crores of rupees. The total addressable market for defence startups is therefore a lucrative investment that must be leveraged effectively to protect India's IP.

In general, however, and in any domain, not necessarily even connected with the defence and military establishment, a war mindset is a must; we need to come out of our sluggish approach that has slowed the MSME sector for many decades. This is the need of the hour. With brilliant minds from every region migrating to limited Tech hubs or indeed, out of the country itself, it is imperative that the industrial ecosystems need to reorganise themselves to new opportunities. Talent needs to identify opportunity, and in return, opportunity must ignite talent. This must be prioritised over all else. Basically, this amounts to a cultural reset for our MSME, industrial, academic and investor institutions.

Finally, we address the matter of self realisation as it relates to entrepreneurship. This is relevant because at the core of entrepreneurship is a confidence that can only come from a certain degree of self-awareness. In times of war, this self-realisation can and must only become more robust. Even with the highest potential and capability, Arjuna did not have integrity of purpose on the eve of the war. Only this could lead to clarity and coherent action on his part. For him to acquire this and carry out his dharma, it needed The Creator Himself to remove the shadows of doubt that had come upon the highest warrior on the planet at the time. As for integrity, it is immanent in an individual and war is a mere test of its manifestation. It matters not if one is in a classroom, a boardroom or a war room.

What a war needs is warriors. Will the MSMEs and VCs of today's Bhārat rise to the occasion?

The Future

Finally, let's go to the future, always a relaxing pastime because no one holds it against you if you're wrong and you have everything to gain if you are right. I am bullish on Bhārat and this has nothing to do with the BJP or Modi. Ours is a country whose time has come, and no adversary, circumstance or obstacle can stop its rise. Finally, we seem to have unshackled ourselves from the tragedies of history that kept us in enslavement and servitude for a millennium. Medium term predictions are the best for commentators and analysts. Short term predictions, even if they are correct, have little shelf life and are best handled by politicians and defence experts. Long term predictions are properly left to visionaries and seers. The medium term, and by this I mean the coming decade, by the end of which we could be a $10 trillion economy, offers the best scope for analysts like me to make intelligent conjectures that can educate people and guide decision makers. It is in this spirit that I have included some recent optimistic pieces that conclude this work.

The first piece in this section was written in unusual circumstances. Firstpost asked me for an article welcoming 2024 on the evening of 26 December 2023 and wanted the piece in 24 hours. As is my wont in late December, I was in Madras for the music season and indeed in the (now politically notorious) Music Academy listening to a vocal music concert when I got the invitation. The article was written (in two stages, during two concerts that evening) on my smartphone and duly sent off on the 27 December (I always like to sleep over a piece) and appeared in Firstpost on the 28 December.

Welcoming 2024: How India Is Experiencing a Silent 'Triveni' Revolution in Politics, Science and Civilisation

Firstpost, 28 December 2023

Summary: Political, economic, and civilisational streams of thought and action have intertwined such that India is becoming Bhārat—a new, more confident, and self-assured nation that is preparing for its 'Amrit Kaal' moment by 2047.

Revolutions are mostly bloody and abrupt. There is a seething undercurrent in the people and when a man of the hour appears, not generally by design but through a confluence of coincidences and circumstances, he sets off cataclysmic changes that overturn many, if not most, of the instrumentalities of the *ancien régime.*

Modern history, and by that I mean the period over the last 500 years, has witnessed many such violent changes that fundamentally changed the lives of common people. Typical examples are the French, American and Russian Revolutions. Other political changes in the last century that have not been given this 'revolution' epithet would certainly qualify for it, for example the regime changes in Turkey, China, Iran, Afghanistan and the USSR.

Other revolutions are more silent but their effects are as momentous. These, for the most part, are somewhat apolitical—the Industrial Revolution and the Silicon Revolution being the most important ones in recent times.

The independence of India was a political event of course but it was relatively bloodless except for the fallout of the partition. Its significance lay in that it triggered a chain reaction in Asia and Africa that resulted in the dismantling of Europe's 500 year colonial enterprise, leading eventually to its ongoing economic collapse.

In post-independence India we have associated colours like green, white, pink and blue with various revolutions that have had transformational economic impacts and improved the quality of life for countless millions.

India is witnessing another silent revolution today, and one that may be more accurately termed a triple revolution, a Triveni moment as it were.

Political, economic and civilisational streams of thought and action have intertwined such that India is becoming Bharat—a new, more confident and self-assured nation, which is preparing for its Amrit Kaal moment by, let us say, 2047.

India's present spurt in economic growth is an outcome of many facilitating financial and fiscal systems being overhauled and reimagined, laying the foundation for sustained increases in prosperity. Digital payments, in which we are clearly the world leader, and the digital India initiative which has seen its moment in the G20 declaration, are clearly moves made by a country that can project itself confidently to be the author of the next generation of global digital public architecture and become the world's third largest economy by say, 2030.

Politically, we have matured considerably since 2014, as the merits of our constitution have begun to sink in because a single party, the Bharatiya Janata Party, has had a simple majority in the Lok Sabha for nearly a decade now. The confusing coalition era, where sleazy compromises between coalition partners were mistakenly, even deliberately, conflated with an idea that finds no mention in our constitution—federalism—is an easily forgotten nightmare.

A majority-driven parliamentary democracy, which is what the makers of our constitution envisaged for us, has finally taken root in our country, even as we will surely witness the political consolidation of a national alternative to the BJP and the decline and disappearance of small, hereditary, regional parties which have hitherto enjoyed undeserved power and pelf through their suffocating control of small caste and sectarian groups in a corruption-ridden pseudo-socialist scarcity economy.

An unexpected focussing of the Triveni of ideas and actions was witnessed in 2023, in the area of science, technology and engineering, with the successful completion of the Chandrayaan-3 mission to the moon, and the Aditya L-1 mission for the observation of the solar corona.

These endeavours have seen a long and laborious gestation, not uncommon in big scientific ventures, but what is unique here is that Bharat has sought and won a place for itself at the high table of the strategically critical area of space research.

Revolutions that are silent sometimes reveal themselves in a single non sequitur happening, and when our moonlander safely placed itself on the hitherto unexplored South Pole of the moon, the whole country sensed and knew that its moment had arrived.

The successful placement of the Aditya capsule in the Lagrange point for solar corona observation a few weeks later showed that these scientific efforts were not fluke events. A country that is economically and politically finding its feet will, sooner or later, begin to show itself in the world of science. This happened in Europe, America and China. It is now happening in India.

Our civilisational values are asserting themselves. The whole world has acknowledged the significance of the Chandrayaan-3 and Aditya L-1 missions and has also realised that with successes of this type, the rise of India within the comity of nations is inevitable. It is no longer a matter of if but when. A similar expedition to the moon by Russia, a few weeks before ours, failed.

Shortly after our successful landing, Japan announced its intention to embark on a similar activity. No testimony to our arrival on the world stage is greater, ironically, than the devastating effect that Chandrayaan-3 and Aditya L-1 have wreaked on the psyche of Pakistan.

Collectively, the people there have realised the enormous difference between their failing project born of religious contempt and those from whom they seceded, and there is now no chance ever of them, forever jealous and inimical, catching up.

The quietest aspects of our silent Triveni revolution have occurred in the civilisational sphere. For too long, an ancient, rich and proud civilisation, confident in its knowledge of the ultimate nature of human reality, was suppressed and crushed under the physical and mental yoke of strange aliens who had no concept of the holistic reality of Bharatavarsha.

Perhaps it is this unquenched self-assuredness of Bharatiyas that has led us individually and collectively to a point where our civilizational values are asserting themselves uniquely in synergy with well accepted, contemporary political and economic paradigms. Methodologies for success are common to all countries and cultures. Strategies are not. It is our 5000 year civilisation and only our 5000 year civilisation that can propel us not just to the third place in the world but even higher.

The Sun and the Moon have played a very special role in all civilisations, cultures and countries. The whole world follows either a solar or a lunar calendar (with Bharatiya ones being both simultaneously).

These two heavenly bodies have been held in worshipful esteem as controlling our actions and our minds. Astronomy sharpened the scientific instincts of humans from times past. Eclipses were predicted accurately from antiquity. Chemical elements were found spectroscopically in the solar flares before they were isolated on Planet Earth.

Even within this spectrum of intellectual thought, Bharat has a very special place, at least in the eyes of the majority of its people. Just as we are children of Bharat Mata, it is instructive to recall the lyrics of the Carnatic music composer Muthuswami Dikshitar who refers to Devi, the supreme mother, as *suryāgni chandra mandala madhya vāsini*, the one who resides in the orbs of the sun, fire and moon.

It is in these celestial orbs that Bharat is seeking its place, as we, its citizens, enter a new year with hope and humility.

> *Let's take up an electoral issue that has emerged as a political problem of the first magnitude—delimitation of parliamentary constituencies.*

Go Small, Win Big: How Redrawing State Lines Makes Delimitation Easier

Swarajya, 10 August 2024

Summary: The road to delimitation is paved with political pitfalls, but smaller states could solve that problem.

The Constitution of India describes the country as a union of states, and the Seventh Schedule lays down a clear division of powers and responsibilities. This, in turn, charts out how a state works and what it ought to do.

However, Article 2, which is supposed to define what a state is, remains vague—deliberately or otherwise. Article 2 merely says that "Parliament may by law admit into the Union, or establish, new States [sic] on such terms and conditions as it thinks fit."

To repudiate any hint of sovereignty ascribed (erroneously) to any of the constituent states of Bharat, the word "state" will be used in this article in small letters to describe them. This is to clearly distinguish them from sovereign entities wherein the capitalised appellation "State" is appropriate, as in say "Indian State", to connote the sovereign democratic republic of India, that is Bharat.

All politics boils down to a combination of identity and economics. Identity is what one is, while economics is a part of what one does. Felicity in understanding what one does accompanied by an inability to clearly define what one is, is a characteristic of a complex system. Such systems are widely recognised in science. Our country Bhārat is a textbook example of a complex system. A problem with our constitution is that it attempts to define what a state is through what it does. This is one of several serious problems in our constitution.

Clause 14, Chapter I, Part I of the States Reorganisation Committee Report of 1955 summarises the position pithily: "The existing structure of the States [sic] of the Indian Union is partly the result of accident and the circumstances attending the growth of the British power in India and partly a by-product of the historic process of the integration of former Indian States. The division of India during the British period into British provinces and Indian States was itself fortuitous and had no basis in Indian history."

Language becoming the primary determinant of identity is a recent phenomenon in our civilisational history. It is fully artificial. The partition of Bengal in 1905, and its subsequent reunification in 1911 was also accompanied by the creation of the linguistic provinces of Orissa and Assam. The separation of a Telugu speaking state from the erstwhile Madras Presidency in 1953, and the appearance of Kannada, Marathi and Gujarati speaking states thereafter, established the pattern. Tamil Nadu defaulted into becoming a linguistic state because of the formation of Andhra Pradesh.

The setting up of these linguistic states, intentional or otherwise, by Jawaharlal Nehru was arguably the single biggest political blunder made in post-independence India. Today, this fake linguistic identity has morphed into calls for 'secession' in a North-South divide, aided and abetted by the Congress party and some regional outfits.

Ironically, the first linguistic state formed in independent India, namely Andhra Pradesh, was divided in 2014 into two Telugu speaking states (Andhra Pradesh and Telangana) demonstrating the hollowness of the linguistic state idea in a modern forward looking country.

Historically, Telugu was always the court language and the language of the higher classes in most parts of southern India for at least 1,000 years right down till 1947. It enjoyed a status equal to that of Sanskrit in the fine arts. Inscriptions in Telugu are found in the recently excavated Gyanvapi Vishwanath Mandir and seem to have been inserted there by pilgrims from what would today be northern Karnataka.

Historically speaking, the Telugu language has always been a unifier and not a divider. Language is, in the end, a social convenience and not an identity marker.

The consequences of linguistic states are deleterious in many ways.

1. Large linguistic states have had lopsided developmental trajectories. Karnataka, Maharashtra, Tamil Nadu and West Bengal, each with a huge metro city, are grossly overdependent on the same. Concerns of those who live beyond the shadows of these megacities are eclipsed. This greatly fuels intrastate inequalities.
2. Cultural diversities are smothered by the singular blanket of linguistic uniformity and regions with markedly different dialects (Garhwal and Kumaon; Jammu and Kashmir; Rayalaseema and Andhra) are disturbingly homogenised. In turn, this leads to divisive politics marked by clientelism, casteism, and secessionist subnationalism.
3. The singular stress on language instead of an accommodative multivariate understanding of identity, makes interstate divisions stark instead of being on a continuum, making it easier to divide Indians rather than uniting them.

At this time, an independent issue is to have a delimitation of parliamentary and assembly constituencies to make our parliamentary democracy more fair and representative. This has been alluded to several times in the recent past by the central government. The construction of a new parliament building with the capability of seating 888 members in the lower house is a hint in this direction.

These two independent issues, namely delimitation of Lok Sabha constituencies and reorganisation of states, may be profitably linked for the furtherance of our democracy.

At the outset, the frozen number of 543 seats in the Lok Sabha is violative of Article 14, i.e. equality before law and equal protection of the law.

This number is not sacrosanct, and has been arrived at by successive delimitations until 1976, which ensured that each MP in the Lok Sabha represents roughly an equal number of citizens. Reality is quite far from this ideal scenario; some Indians thus get to have greater say in the running of this country, flying in the face of equality of citizens.

As per the Election Commission of India, the five largest parliamentary constituencies of the country in terms of number of electors constitute 1,16,51,249 electors taken together, while the smallest five together have 7,56,820 electors. The total electorate size in the largest five is thus 15.4 times of that in the smallest five. We may term this as a "skew ratio". These skewed numbers show that the electoral significance of a vote can differ significantly from one constituency to another.

Additionally, if one takes the voting population of India as 97 crore, then there are on average 17 lakh voters represented by each Lok Sabha member currently. This number is way too large and it means that an individual voter has, for all practical purposes, lost any direct contact with the person he or she has elected to the Lok Sabha.

Based on the number of seats in the new parliament building, one might assume that there will be 888 Lok Sabha members in a Lower House constituted after a nationwide delimitation exercise.

In such an event, one arrives at an average figure of 10 lakh voters per constituency, which appears to be more reasonable. However, if this exercise is done proportionately (1 constituency today becomes 1.69 constituencies after delimitation), the skew ratio still stays high, meaning that the value of an individual vote will still remain widely different in different parts of the country.

Alternatively, if the exercise is carried out population wise, there will be a marked decrease in the representation of the southern states.

Both methods are therefore unsatisfactory. Any increase in the number of constituencies must therefore be accompanied by a complete redrawing of limits so that there are just around 10 lakh voters in each and every new constituency in the country with the skew ratio approaching 1.00. However, even this is not enough, given the present structuring of the states.

This is so because the connection between any future parliamentary delimitation exercise and the manner and way in which states of the Indian Union have been defined by Parliament would still remain tenuous.

The present 28 states and eight Union Territories (UT) are shockingly different in size. These differences are partly on account of former historical events, and partly on account of a reluctance by some, mostly in the larger (linguistic) states, to consider division of their states into smaller, more governable units, blocking such moves and using language as a convenient excuse.

The recent gymnastics in Karnataka with respect to quotas for Kannada speaking employees in private industry is a case in point. A comprehensive reorganisation of states is, however, almost mandatory today and unless this exercise is done ab initio it will lack objectivity and rationality. It cannot be done incrementally.

Such reorganisation should smoothly dovetail into the parliamentary delimitation exercise, so that each newly constituted state has more or less equal representation in the new parliament. The question of larger states dominating the political discourse would be then relegated to history.

Projected 75 states of Nayā Bhārat

Uttar Pradesh might be accused today by Tamil Nadu of dominating it in certain ways, but it is hardly likely that a Kongu Nadu would similarly accuse an equally populated Awadh. No new state would be affected by so-called North-South demographic differences, because all states would have nearly the same population, and thus a roughly equal say in the trajectory of the country.

In this way, two independent phenomena, namely delimitation and states reorganisation, would be brought together synergistically. Simultaneously, the unhealthy concentration of resources, political power, and opportunities in singular megacities can be checked, resulting in a more equal distribution of prosperity. Likewise, economic policymaking becoming more decentralised can enable regions to specialise in goods and services as per their competencies, unimpeded from distant state capitals which remain less than responsive to such demands.

Delimitation and States Reorganization

Esamskriti.com, 24 March 2025

Summary: An Indic solution to Delimitation concerns.

Who says Sanātana Dharma is not a political religion? From the earliest days of our civilization, our scriptures have dwelt upon the rights and responsibilities of our ruling classes and how they are accountable to the people they rule. They are, however, also accountable to a higher call—the call of dharma, which is the sovereign of sovereigns: *dharmam kshatrasya kshatram*, so says the Brihadāranyaka Upanishad.

Recent times have seen an unusual and peculiar political problem in our country—that of delimitation, an unusual and perhaps little known word at least as far as the average citizen is concerned. We are a democracy, and this means that from time to time, we participate in elections where we vote for candidates in such a way that the one who secures the maximum number of votes in our particular constituency is declared the winner and represents us, the electorate of that particular constituency, in an assembly of legislators, say the Lok Sabha or lower house of parliament. So far so good.

An essential feature of any functioning democracy, and India does consider itself one, is that the value of any vote anywhere in the country in being able to elect a representative to the Lok Sabha should be the same. It sounds simple but in India this simple idea has become complicated because for a full 50 years, the delimitation exercise has been frozen, in other words the sizes of the constituencies have not been continuously modified to take into account the changes in population within that particular constituency.

Because of the freeze, constituencies where the rate of population growth has been relatively high have ended up being systematically under-represented in the Lok Sabha. Typically, these constituencies are found in the northern states, for example Uttar Pradesh and Bihar.

Conversely, states with lower rates of population growth are over-represented. Tamil Nadu is a notable example, and today a vote in this state is worth roughly 1.6 votes in say, Rajasthan.

Delimitations are carried out in democracies on the basis of the latest census that has been carried out in that country. Here, another problem crops up for us—the last census was held in 2011 i.e. fifteen years ago. The census that would normally have been carried out in 2021 was held in abeyance because of the Covid pandemic. So any delimitation exercise we carry out today must be on the basis of a new census, or we shall have to compromise and use the population figures of the 2011 census.

Delimitation has become a pressing political problem because the two groups of states, northern and southern, have entirely different opinions as to how the exercise is to be carried out.

The northern states have not said so explicitly but they would clearly prefer if our constituencies are delimited on the basis of population—as is done in any functioning democracy in the world. The principle here is: Each Vote, Same Value. Conversely, the southern states wish to retain their representational advantage, as it stood when the freeze was first put in place in 1976, and simply increase the number of constituencies all over in a proportional manner. In this proposal, any constituency would be delimited so that it becomes 1.58

constituencies, and effectively our 543 Lok Sabha members would become 858 members reflecting the population increase over 40 years, namely from 1971 to 2011.

Ideally, however, each state of the Union must enjoy the same heft with the central government: Each State Same Heft. The southern formulation not only contradicts this but goes further and asserts that the smaller southern states must enjoy greater heft simply because they are special. Some southerners even say that delimitation should follow from economic status: those states who have contributed more to the economy should have a greater say in the legislative business of the country. The meaning of the word 'delimitation' itself seems to be changing!

Both solutions will raise more problems.

The suggestion based on population is constitutionally correct and mathematically flawless but it will increase the heft of large heavily populated northern states in parliament contradicting the principle of Each State Same Heft. The suggestion based on proportionality is plain incorrect, and worse still, illogical. If this suggestion made by the southern states is accepted, the asymmetry that has arisen because of the 50 year freeze will only get amplified further; effectively it is equivalent to imposing another 25 year freeze, and indeed this is what the chief minister of Tamil Nadu is implying. By 2051 when a new freeze expires, we would effectively have ceased being a democracy, in any understood sense of the term.

There is no way in which the twin conditions of Each Vote Same Value and Each State Same Heft are satisfied unless Bhārat is reformulated in terms of nearly equally populated smaller states that are in themselves defined keeping in mind historical, geographical, economic, cultural, linguistic and civilisational criteria.

An organic formulation of seventy-five states is shown in the map below and has been arrived at naturally without any artificial contrivance. The best argument or proof for our conjecture is a visual one—behold! A justification is provided in our recently published book that is mentioned at the end of this article but any Bharatiya will recognise that these divisions are a truer representation of our identities than the twenty-eight state model that we have at present.

The structuring of our present 28 states and 8 Union Territories is irrational, even eccentric, and has no basis in the history, geography, culture and economics of our ancient land, Bhāratavarsha. It was a cut-and-paste hotchpotch of boundaries that had been hastily and arbitrarily drawn up by our colonial masters overlaid with a crazy quilt of 564 Princely States that were defined and orchestrated by them to maintain their effective suzerainty over their Indian Empire. To add insult to injury we further compromised our map in 1956 with the introduction of linguistic states, another British concept that set Indian against Indian using the fake concept of linguistic identity.

If we have seventy-five states of nearly equal population of 2 crore each, we naturally arrive at a situation where each of these small states will send 12 elected representatives to the Lok Sabha in a lower house of 858 members. There is no question of any north-south divide because there will be no north and no south, just 75 logically obtained domains that have their culture encoded from the past and their economy beckoning to the future. India of the past will become Bhārat of the future.

One may only ponder as to why these seventy-five political entities appeared so naturally, almost affirming our past and our Sanātani culture that upholds Dharma above all else. The number 75 immediately leads to an average population of 2 crore for these states, a number that is eminently governable with no rancour and ill-will among states.

The only ones who would stoutly defend the present 28 state dispensation would be the entrenched political classes who have built up financial empires based on caste calculations within states as defined presently.

This confluence of politics and dharma, unique to Bhārat, is already foretold in Verse 165 of one of our most ancient hymns, the Lalita Sahasranama where the Supreme Goddess is invoked thus:

Dharmādhārā dhan'ādhyakshā dhana-dhānya-vivardhinī

Salutations to Her who carries Dharma of the Universe. Salutations to Her who controls all riches. Salutations to Her who increases riches and harvests. Salutations to Her who brought together this conjunction of politics and dharma to further the economic prosperity of Her chosen land.

> *Let's move to the so-called language issue, which is a consequence of linguistic states and the 50 year delimitation freeze. The clumsy directive in Maharashtra to make Hindi a compulsory third language is divisive in the extreme, and has brought bitter political rivals together. I would like to make my own opinion on this matter crystal clear: In no state where a non-Hindi language is dominant, should Hindi be introduced at any level in any educational institution as a compulsory language with an examination that the student has to take. Hindi is not our national language. Bhārat has no national language and does not need one. Hindi is an informal link language and is used by people in non-Hindi speaking states as a matter of convenience when the circumstances demand it. The BJP, rightly or wrongly, has now become associated with imposition of Hindi on people who do not want it. The party will pay an electoral price if it does not seek to dispel this perception.*

Tower of Babel: Languages Are No Longer Impenetrable Silos That Divide People

CNN News 18, 1 June 2025

Summary: The need for a formal link language is not as acute as it was in say 1950 when linguistic groups were sharply demarcated

We commend the recent decision of the CBSE to make instruction in the local language, mostly the mother tongue, mandatory at the primary level. The board has directed all affiliated schools to begin mapping students' mother tongues "at the earliest" and realign instructional materials accordingly before the end of the summer break.

The issue of medium of instruction in education continues to seize the imagination of students, teachers, parents, and educationists. It is a matter fraught with political connotations. The recurrent bouts of Hindi hatred that grip parts of the country from time to time are stark reminders that the country remains ill at ease on the issue of language. Changing economic realities have only morphed the issue over time, instead of eradicating it.

The National Educational Policy (NEP) 2020 identifies issues and analyses various schemes that have been operating so far. Rather vaguely, it says that "the three-language formula will continue to be implemented while keeping in mind the constitutional provisions, aspirations of the people, regions, and the Union, and the need to promote multilingualism as well as promote national unity". In this laundry list of irreconcilables, one wonders what purpose did this sentence serve, if any. Any policy document, including the NEP, places a burden of intellectual and methodological clarity on the authors, for the government is expected to heed to their counsel. If the government is unable to coherently respond to the issue at hand, a large part of the blame lies on those passing off avoidance as advice.

India does not have a national language and rightly so. A polyglot country like ours does not need one. A European-style nation-state requires a certain ethnic and linguistic homogeneity to function; a civilisational state like ours is bound together with shared practices, worldviews, and philosophical approaches to our place as individuals within the society and of our nation in the world, instead of just language. Telugu signboards in Ayodhya and Shri Venkateshwara being worshipped in Uttarakhand are not contradictions of any kind — it's simply how our civilisation works, and it is through a healthy appreciation of diversity that a sense of kinship and bonding is established.

Our Constitution recognises 22 official languages and some combination of these is used by the Union and state governments in their work. The constitutionally mandated dictum of installing Hindi as the sole official language for the Union is a dead letter. Likewise, demanding some sacred enshrinement to any language is absurd. Let it be abundantly clear – linguistic chauvinism has gone hand in hand with separatism in this country, and it is not surprising that issues surrounding language crop up whenever national security has been under threat.

Indeed, the evolution of linguistic supremacists in India count in their august lineage the Pakistan movement and its fascination with

Urdu, the Dravidians of Tamil Nadu who were out-and-out separatists and committed genocide on Brahmins, and the murderous insurgents of Assam and Meghalaya who ethnically cleansed Bengali populations. Under the guise of 'self respect', the agenda to soft-balkanise India was given wind. Alloyed with linguistic demands are other destructive ideas such as India being labelled a 'federation', by a repeated regurgitation of India being a Union of states; never mind Ambedkar's clear and unambiguous utterances on India not being a federation in any true sense:

"The federation is a union because it is indestructible. Although the country and the people may be divided into different states for convenience of administration, the country is one integral whole, its people a single people living under a single imperium derived from a single source."

The subservience to the single source, ie, the Sanātani substratum animating Bhārat's sense of self (beyond the gilded asylums of anti-India enclaves dotting our metro cities), and the single imperium derived therefrom, ie, Bhārat, overrides all other considerations. As Himanta Biswa Sarma aptly articulated, it is only the civilisation which gives any meaning, and space to operate, to the Constitution—civilisation first, Constitution follows. Linguistic subversiveness cannot be tolerated.

The single most important objective for India, if one takes a higher level view, is to build on its economic growth and solve the jobs crisis. Whether it is our physical safety, in the form of military deterrence, or to ensure a comfortable standard of living for all our denizens, the economic rise of the country is a sine qua non. The logic of how we approach our linguistic diversity needs to be rescued from the clutches of fanatical, ideologically obsessed experts and soft-secessionists, and be viewed pragmatically from the lens of economic, and underlying civilisational, utility.

As India strives to ascend in the comity of nations, it is clear that our huge numbers of children and young adults of school and college-going age should be optimally advantaged in order that they are able to cope and compete within their state, country, and internationally. The entire issue of language should be moved from the emotional to the pragmatic. Language is a matter of utility, communicability and practicality. Our educational policies should be framed accordingly, and the Central Board of Secondary Education (CBSE) has made the right move at the right time.

This leveraging is most effectively done linguistically: a child should be taught basic concepts in the language in which he or she can best emote and can give free rein to imagination. More so, each language is closely intertwined with the land, its people, their culture, and their myriad thought patterns, which have to be developed for intellectual diversity and leveraged by the nation at large. The NEP discreetly speaks of "home language/mother tongue/local language/regional language". Let us not forget that for the vast majority, all these languages are one and the same.

It is important that our young people are equipped to excel in imaginative skills because it is such skills that are sorely lacking in our outmoded rote learning method of education today. Accordingly, there can be no doubt that education in the foundational stage, as defined in NEP, namely ages three to eight, must be in the local language with no exception. By no exception, we mean no exception. Don't speak about children of transferable central government employees. They are a miniscule minority for which a special solution can be worked out. The minority should not dictate to the majority who belong to the state, were born in the state and will live in their state for most of their lives. Ideally, education in the local language should also continue into the preparatory (8-11), middle (11-14) and secondary (14-18) stages with other languages. The CBSE's recent decision to implement education in the mother tongue must be lauded in this regard. There is little doubt that the imaginative skill of an individual is enhanced if basic education is imparted in the mother tongue. The first language is the language of the land, and is the language of thought.

The second language, a civilisational language, again without any exception, has to be Sanskrit. India's civilisational ethos cannot be compromised any longer, and the children of Bharat deserve to draw on the vast knowledge of their ancestors, and put an end to the pretence that we are simply brown sahebs. No arguments of minorityism or ethnic origin can override this imperative. This will be the fulcrum of true national integration, for this not only connects languages, but connects a citizen with his civilisational continuity, and his indigenous systems of knowledge and governance, ushering in decolonisation in a true sense. The language can be appropriately introduced as the civilisational language everywhere at the preparatory stage (age 8).

English is our pathway to the world. It is also a sort of link language within the country although Hindi is fast replacing it in this regard. English should be deromanticised, and approached as a technical language. Technical and professional, instead of literary proficiency, should be the goal. The language has to be approached merely as an instrument, which will not only contribute to decolonisation without loss of a global outlook, but improve standards where they matter the most. English is still essential, however, and increased felicity in this wonderful international language needs to be developed in order that we can compete aggressively in the metropolitan and international arenas. It can and should come in as the technical language everywhere at the middle stage (age 11).

In short, our so-called three-language formula, and similar formulaic prescriptions may be gently allowed to lapse. They were useful in the interim but will hardly be so in the long run.

The need for a formal link language is, however, not as acute as it was in say 1950 when linguistic groups were sharply demarcated. Television, movies and social media, and also the migration of people across the country have ensured that many residents in urban and semi-urban areas have some sort of working knowledge of both English and Hindi. People from outside a state also seem to be readily picking up the local language even when it is quite distinct from their mother tongue, due to purely economic reasons. One hears a lot more Hindi in Chennai and Bengaluru today than one did 10 years ago. At the same time, one hears north Indians in the southern states speaking the local language in shops and restaurants. Languages are no longer impenetrable silos that divide people. Languages unite, and the pursuit of prosperity unites even further.

> *This matter of Hindi has continued to worry me in the past few months. Is it being really imposed on the southern states as it is made out to be, or is there a sizable section of north Indians who associate Indian identity with Hindi, Hindu and Hindustan?*

Is Hindi a Marker of National Identity?

CNN News 18, 4 August 2025

Summary: The status of Hindi in Bhārat today is unusual. It is definitely some kind of a linking language, if it is not exactly a link language.

Bhārat, that is India, is a country now in a critical period in its history where it is seeking an identity which will become ineluctable in its advancement into nationhood. A national identity includes people with that identity and excludes those who do not. Both these inclusionary and exclusionary attributes qualify any nation, however defined, and whether it is or not congruent with a country. Markers of identity in Bhārat could be one of many: religion, bloodline, domicile, culture, geography, diet, history, economics, and finally, and contentiously, language.

Language is a social necessity because its use is the easiest way for an individual to communicate with his or her neighbour. It is defined by necessity — a necessity to communicate. If it is required for an individual to communicate with another individual, they will construct a common language to do so. Language, therefore, is formed as a link between individuals as a matter of practicality, and usually it is a matter of convenience and common sense.

The origin of a language is therefore rarely emotional. Language is not an emotive issue, and yet it has seemingly become one in contemporary India, with some states feeling that their identity is being threatened. This is not a purely Indian issue — the Catalans, Basques, Ukrainians, Romansch and Maoris have all been through this emotional wringer and yet have not succumbed to centrifugal pressures.

India is a polyglot country. There are many languages spoken all over the subcontinent, from Brahui to Bihari to Beary, and if one counts all the myriad dialects and variations that constitute our micro diversity tapestry, one will run into several thousands of them. Out of this linguistic panorama, let us address the question as to whether one of them, namely a language we call Hindi, is the natural marker of our national identity as Bhāratiyas.

Hindi, as we understand it, is the language that is used in the newspapers, media and various types of documentation. It is easier to define it in its written form rather than through its spoken variations. As spoken, it is hardly defined in a sharp manner. It is a hybrid – to use scientific jargon, it is a linear combination of several linguistic components with variable coefficients. The Hindi that is spoken in Kashi, Ayodhya and Mathura, to take these cities as mere examples, is different. Moving into an outer arc, these varieties of Hindi are different from those that are commonly used in, say, Chandigarh, Bhopal and Patna.

Let us also not forget that the Hindi which is spoken today in our country and what one might attempt to make a marker of national identity has also evolved from something called Hindustani that was widely understood in the northern parts of undivided India, after culling words and phrases from Urdu, another hybrid with a Persian component that served and, to some extent, still serves the needs of Muslims in India. Indonesia and Turkey made similar attempts to 'homogenise' a national language with mixed success.

In summary, Hindi cannot even be defined as a single language, and any attempt to sanitise it towards trying to make it a national identity marker will inevitably disturb and eventually destroy the fabric of micro-diversity that has evolved naturally in Hindi — as a social necessity — within the group of Hindi speakers that stands today at a mind-blowing 60 crore in India, conservatively speaking.

The status of Hindi in Bhārat today is unusual. It is definitely some kind of a linking language, if it is not exactly a link language. In this respect, it shares many features with English, which is also a linking language — the only difference being that Hindi and English link different sets of people. Both languages are highly useful and important in that they help to bring people together in a country where there are so many factors that tend to tear people apart.

The formation of linguistic states in independent India after 1953 (Orissa was the first linguistic state and was created by the British in 1916) was a singularly ill-conceived decision that was taken as a knee-jerk reaction to an immediate political crisis brought about by a hunger strike by a single individual leading to his death after eleven days. Linguistic states were roundly criticised in 1955 by Ambedkar, who viewed them as facilitating Balkanisation and divisions within the country. Subsequent events have proved him, sadly enough, to have been unerringly accurate.

We face today the spectre of states like Maharashtra, Karnataka, Gujarat, Tamil Nadu, and West Bengal that are *politically empowered linguistic entities* within the Union of India. These states go against Ambedkar's wise dictum that one must have a single language spoken in any given state but that one must never have a state defined in such a way that all people who speak a single language must belong to it. Effectively, language that had only communicability among individuals as its motivation has morphed into an emotional issue with deleterious socio-economic consequences.

It was possible for many in the Hindi-speaking areas of the country to disregard the so-called Hindi-imposition problem as a peculiarity of Tamil Nadu and its supposedly jingoistic tendencies or of West Bengal with its long and shambolic tradition of opposing anything from Delhi as an infringement on the so-called independence of Bengal. Karnataka too has recently joined this club of linguistic naysayers with the more drastic add-on that no language other than Kannada will be tolerated in this state; any language other than Kannada, except Urdu, is being considered an imposition. Why Urdu should be acceptable while Hindi is not is beyond the comprehension of at least this author. Let us just say that language has become an entirely political issue.

The recent happenings in Maharashtra have taken the language issue into new and disturbing dimensions. Here, the championing of the Marathi language has brought two feuding cousins together on the same political platform after 20 years of not communicating with one another in any way whatsoever. This is a political message to the Bharatiya Janata Party (BJP) and its parent organisation, the Rashtriya Swayamsevak Sangh (RSS), and any member of the group that was sarcastically termed "Hindiwallahs" by TT Krishnamachari in the Constituent Assembly debates (1946-1950). Let us make no mistake about the latest political developments in Maharashtra. This Hindiwallah group had issued a clarion call in the constituent assembly debates for a unitary structure for the country, with Hindi, Hindu, and Hindustan being its main, exclusionary themes. It is well known that the debate on a national language and Hindi numerals was the lengthiest of the debates. Finally, it was decided after two full days of debate that India would not have a national language; Hindi and English became primary co-equals among the 22 official languages in the Eighth Schedule of our Constitution.

Why is Maharashtra important in a way that Tamil Nadu, Karnataka and West Bengal are not with respect to the so-called Hindi imposition by the central government? Marathi is an Indo-European language that shares many linguistic and etymological features with Hindi. It shares the Nagari script too, unlike Gujarati, Punjabi, and Bengali, other Indo-European languages that are also related to Hindi.

According to the 2011 Census of India, approximately 81.26 per cent of the population in Maharashtra speaks Marathi as their first, second or third language. As both Marathi and Hindi are Indo-European languages derived from Sanskrit, with the further influence of Hindi through media and Bollywood, education and migration, it is likely that a majority of Marathi speakers have a working knowledge of Hindi. Without precise census data isolating Marathi speakers' proficiency in Hindi, a conservative estimate based on the linguistic and cultural context would place a figure of 70-90 per cent of Marathi speakers having a knowledge of Hindi. As additional information, 42 per cent of native Hindi speakers in Maharashtra know Marathi.

With so much linguistic similarity between Marathi and Hindi, the emotional reaction of Maharashtrians to the introduction of Hindi as a compulsory subject in Class I and beyond is an unexpected development and warrants close attention by the political class. This reaction should not snowball into a wider conflict that affects all non-Hindi-speaking states, even threatening the unity and integrity of Bhārat. This is as clear a signal as a political signal can get, and it would be foolhardy of the BJP and RSS to ignore it.

The National Education Policy (NEP) 2020 has talked about the medium of education in schools in terms of the three-language formula, but what these three languages will be and whether they will be uniform in all or most of the states is left unsaid. Little is mentioned in NEP about how all its recommendations (including the ones on language) are ever going to be implemented. This is the biggest, even catastrophic, deficiency in the document and one which can even render the entire NEP nugatory.

As an immediate stopgap measure (ad hoc, really), the central government would do well to announce that Hindi will not be a medium of instruction in a non-Hindi speaking state, at any level, without the express concurrence of the state in question to so include it. How the rest of the 3-language formula is to be implemented, whether it should be a 2-language formula or whether we do not even need any 'formula' for language in a polyglot country, will be a matter for further mature discussion. For now, the immediate priority is to cool the political temperatures south of the Vindhyas so that this discussion on Hindi ceases forthwith.

Hindi is not a marker of national identity, and any attempt to force-feed this language to large numbers of non-Hindi-speaking people will only lead to deleterious consequences for the BJP at the hustings.

> *To change tack, another matter of great significance in our geostrategic calculations for the medium term future is how Bhārat can secure its supply chains for the Rare Earth Elements (REE). This subject holds a special interest for me because I am a research chemist and can understand the incredible sophistry that is involved in exploiting a specific property of a specific REE to fabricate a highly specific device that does not have an alternative. My forthcoming book on supply chains and my background as a research chemist have prompted me to think a great deal of these REE metals that have become so very important in geopolitics and geostrategies today—every country wants to stockpile REE, but for now, only China seems to have a strategic advantage.*

Can Bhārat Do It from Mines to Magnets with Rare Earths?

ETGovernment, 27 June 2025

At the time of writing, an all-out crisis grips our vaunted automotive industry. The sudden imposition of Chinese export and re-export controls on its rare earths products has threatened entire assembly lines with suspension of production, and looming layoffs. This industry is not only a top foreign exchange earner, but is also one of our most sophisticated manufacturing ecosystems, having large overlaps with high-technology strategic sectors such as defense and aerospace. Electronics production, which has been nurtured and scaled over the past few years, may be next in line to face a crunch. Any prolonged restrictions on rare earth supplies may cause long-term damage to many of our complex supply chains, derailing our economic growth and supply chain resilience for years to come. Embarrassingly, delegations of our industrialists are supplicating before Chinese authorities to obtain critical imports. It is not that we do not have rare earth reserves, nor was the crippling dependence on Chinese imports unknown to us. For the sorry situation we are battling today, we have only ourselves to blame.

The rare earths are a group of 17 metals in the periodic table: lanthanum, the 14 elements that follow it horizontally, and scandium and yttrium, which precede it vertically. Notably, lithium, a fairly commonly found metal (unlike what most people believe), is not a rare earth. These elements have tantalisingly similar properties, making their separation, purification, and processing an exacting (and polluting) technological process. Yet, in most of their important properties which find application today, interchanging them is not possible. Each of these elements has distinctive attributes that cannot be generally replicated by other elements. Exploiting their minute differences (which exist mostly in their optical and magnetic attributes) has led to the ever-expanding cornucopia of advanced technology. Anything with a chip in it—from a mobile phone to a nuclear submarine or the advanced seekers in the missiles used during Operation Sindoor—would be impossible to make without rare earths. The relative importance of access to high-quality rare earths will only increase, because technological development has adopted a trajectory that depends on exploiting the peculiar properties of individual rare earths. Reverting to our beleaguered automotive industry, an average car requires a large palette of rare earths, including around 2.2 kgs of cerium. To put it simply, modern technology, of any kind and across all sectors, is impossible without rare earths.

China is the world's largest supplier of rare earths across mining, refining, and recycling. However, it is not due to any natural advantages it has per se—rare earths are neither rare, nor are they 'earths', and their reserves are more or less a function of the size of a country's geographical area. Thus, geographically expansive countries, such as the USA, Russia, China, Canada, South Africa and Australia, will have known (and sizable) reserves of rare earths. India, too, likewise, is estimated to have the world's third-largest reserves of rare earths, notwithstanding that our geography is so poorly explored and prospected for rare earths that presently known reserves will be a mere fraction of the mineral wealth it actually possesses. What makes China so special?

Initially, the USA was in pole position concerning rare earths. Deng Xiaoping, the architect of the modern Chinese economy, was anxious to develop supply chains, which would give Chinese manufacturing an unbeatable cost advantage, and could provide it with leverage over other countries. He specifically identified rare earths as a strategic sector and marshalled resources to incentivise mining and refining capabilities, beginning with the '863' program in 1986. Of critical importance to the Chinese was to develop separation and purification capabilities at a massive scale, such that a relative cost advantage could be developed that could not be bridged by competitors without sustained subsidies. China's (till-recent) disregard for environmental concerns, coupled with its tendency to engage in dumping products below production cost to bankrupt competition from time to time, has cemented its position of dominance. Mining rare earths, as such, is not a critical or complex activity; China concentrates more on separation, refining, and finished products. Thus, while the Chinese share in the low-margin activity of mining rare earths has consistently come down and stands at around 60% of global supply, its prowess in separation and purification is at a whopping 91% of global output for rare earths used in magnets (neodymium, praseodymium, dysprosium, terbium, etc.). China has also nurtured the world's largest cadre of rare earth scientists, and has dedicated institutions to research and develop related technologies. This mastery over rare earths has greatly helped China in other fields, since rare earth-related research dovetails neatly with renewable energy and rechargeable batteries, and thus, Japanese industry faced severe pressures during the 2011 flare-up of the Senkaku Islands dispute, when China halted rare earth exports. We faced a similar situation soon after Operation Sindoor.

The world had taken notice years ago. The USA's Department of Defence is enabling a mines-to-magnets supply chain by restarting closed mines and building lost infrastructure, and Europe is poised to have three different rare earths refining facilities by 2030. Australia has also joined the fray and is collaborating with the USA. Bharat chose the path of consistent neglect, despite warnings. In fact, the authors have been raising the alarm since 2022, providing detailed policy suggestions grounded in scientific realities. Until disaster visited our doorsteps, the governmental outlook was lackadaisical at best.

India was, ironically, a pioneer in rare earths production. IREL (India) Limited, originally India Rare Earths Limited, was set up in 1950 itself, tasked with developing rare earth products. A policy error that lasted decades came soon after—IREL was placed under the Department of Atomic Energy, and rare earths that occurred along with radioactive thorium in Bharat's monazite sands were irrationally monopolised by IREL, locking out private investment. The reader will note that thorium is not a rare earth. Only recent amendments, beginning in 2023, have seen a partial undoing of this grave folly. IREL, too, has been utterly neglectful of rare earths at large and has little to show for except exporting away partially processed ores (only for us to then import finished products). Some puzzling choices were also proceeded with in the interim—for example, instead of focusing on the mines-to-magnet supply chains of critical industrial magnets based on neodymium, IREL intended to set up a samarium-cobalt magnet manufacturing facility in 2018, without first perfecting the separation and processing of samarium, and knowing fully well that we have no current primary source of domestic cobalt. That is another matter: production did not commence until 2025 and has not been scaled up as yet. Similarly, the exploration of the country for valuable rare earths remained a marginal activity and remained fragmented across a cacophony of government agencies and PSUs. India's auction-based mine allocation system, designed to maximise State revenue, does not permit a private entity to mine a block they may have discovered without an auction, sapping incentives for private exploration. All in all, as the authors have written previously in great detail, Bhārat's rare earths policy framework remains dysfunctional, and industrial capabilities are anaemic at best.

If public reports are to be believed, a few critical suggestions made over the years by the authors, such as focusing on cerium due to its relative abundance and use in the automotive industry, viability gap funding, and making IREL sign agreements to supply non-radioactive partially processed ores to the private sector, are finally being considered. Buoyed at last by a government commitment to provide incentives for rare earth magnet manufacturing, several players, foreign and domestic, are promising much. Are they promising too much? When the overall supply chain of mines to magnets is so pervasively mismanaged, and must contend with an exceedingly prohibitive policy regime, merely setting up manufacturing is akin to pretending that a bandage works just as well as a surgery. To illustrate, one of the proposals supposedly being considered entails a group mining monazite in Sri Lanka (since the same ore, despite its copious occurrence in India, has been unwisely monopolised by IREL), separating and refining it abroad (in all likelihood, China), and then making magnets in India. Such measures, while appreciable to the extent that at least some stretches of the rare earths supply chain come onshore, cannot reduce our China dependence quandary. There are no alternatives to the difficult and dirty chemistry of separation and processing being built up and subsequently backward integrated with an agile mining industry, as well as forward integrated further with competitive user industries. Unsurprisingly, the Ministry of Heavy Industries' Secretary, Kamran Rizvi, is reported to have asked companies to "make realistic statements about magnet production". The word "realistic" is of note here.

Bhārat needs to urgently undertake deep and pervasive reforms, roll out long-term incentives to promote private industrial capabilities in rare earths, and bolster capacity in each stretch of the supply chain (beginning with mining but particularly concentrating on separation and refining) to achieve a competitive mine-to-magnet ecosystem. Anything short of that will only prolong our vulnerability to Chinese pressure. As has been the authors' longstanding recommendation, it is best to concentrate on a select portfolio of rare earths first, such as cerium. India has significant known reserves of cerium. In fact, it holds the fifth-largest rare earth reserves globally, estimated at approximately 6.9 million metric tonnes. These ores occur with ores of neodymium, praseodymium and lanthanum in minerals like monazite and bastnäsite. Our experiences with cerium can then become a template for future rare earth elements' development.

Bhāratiyas must realise that conflicts today are seldom economic or military—they are economic and military. Economics is becoming securitised, and military actions are reattaining their Clausewitzian logic of being politics with other means. The war over rare earths is one such global theatre of warfare, which, unbeknownst to most Bhāratiyas, has reached their borders (if not within our borders already). The incessant conflict in Myanmar, for example, attains a particular salience when one observes that up to 80% of the dysprosium being processed in China may be illegally sourced ores from rebel-held areas in northern Myanmar. Similarly, Balochistan is touted to have significant reserves, with more than one power vying to gain control over the same. The Indian Ocean is rich in nodules that may be mined for rare earths—a fact that may well be appreciated by the increasing American and Chinese naval presence in the region. There have been promising initial finds in Afghanistan as well.

Bhārat has already been too late in this game. It cannot afford to neglect serious and purposeful action regarding rare earths at this critical juncture.

This is a serious matter, and one only hopes that our government is taking it up with the seriousness it deserves.

The following piece on IKS brings together many of the themes I have thought about when I wrote the previous articles: education, colonisation, Bhāratiyatva, our sastras and our geopolitical future.

Indian Knowledge Systems: Bridging Ancient Wisdom and Modern Education in the Journey towards a Civilizational State

The Commune, 19 December 2024

Summary: Indian Knowledge Systems (IKS) represent a repository of indigenous knowledge that remains relevant in modern contexts, such as wellness, sustainability, and interdisciplinary research. IKS is a term that has come into vogue recently and its meaning might be mostly unclear to many lay persons.

What is IKS? Is it a new development in studies of epistemology or is it of ancient provenance? Is it mostly a qualitative and incoherent jumble of superstitions and stories about an imaginary India where everything was just fine? Or were we just untamed savages waiting for the white man to come and educate us and make us civilized and after we got educated, are we trying to imagine something glorious in the past and ascribe everything we know to IKS? Still, others note that the government of a secular country should not indulge itself or support an education system that is rooted solely in the religious and socio-cultural beliefs of one community, namely the Hindus, even if they account for 80% of India's population today. Even here, the naysayers hold that IKS is the property of savarna Hindus, and it is by no means inclusive in nature.

The meaning of IKS can be described by the three words Indian, Knowledge, and Systems. By Indian, we mean the entire land that is called Bhāratvarsha, namely all the land between Kandahar and Mandalay, from the Himalayas to the Indian Ocean, in today's terminology consisting of all countries that are loosely clubbed together as South Asia. This is the geographical sacred space of Sanātana Dharma and when one refers to IKS, one refers to the knowledge systems that were developed and emanated from this sacred space. IKS uniquely belongs to Sanātana Dharma and may be enjoyed and appreciated by all who adhere to the principles of Dharma.

By Knowledge, we mean the entire corpus of written documentation and oral traditions accompanying Sanātana Dharma in addition to various allied bodies of knowledge that have accrued from experiences in day-to-day life, folklore, traditions, and customs that have enabled this sturdy civilization that is going strong after 5000 years, some say possibly longer. The written documentation is based around the 14 knowledge silos or chatrurdasa vidyasthanas, namely the four Vedas, the six darshanas, the epics, and the Puranas.

पुराण न्याय मीमांसा धर्मशास्त्रांग मिश्रिताः।
वेदाः स्थानानि विद्यानाम धर्मस्य च चतुर्दश।।

Purāna nyāya mimāngsā dharmashāstranga mishritāh |
Vedāh sthānani vidyānām dharmasya cha chaturdasha ||

The Vedas are the blueprint and the Vedāngas, literally, the limbs of the Vedas, unlock the Vedas and make them accessible. The six Vedāngas are Siksha, Chhanda, Vyakarana, Nirukta, Jyotisha and Kalpa. These subjects were an integral and essential part of the ancient Vedic education system, aimed to promote an all-round development of the students with a better understanding of the Vedas and Vedic practices. The aspects from the Vedas that lead to better living for all are also a part of the knowledge corpus. These include the medicinal treatises of Chāraka and Susruta, the Arthasāstra of Chānakya, the Patanjali Yoga Sutras, the Kāvyas of Kalidasa and others, Bharatā's Natyasastra, Sārangadeva's Sangita Ratnākara and the Rasa Ratna Samuchchaya of Vāgbhata and Nagārjuna, the study of chemistry and materials. This is just a sampling. There was a time when Sāmaveda, which is just one among the four Vedas, had over a thousand branches! It is practically impossible to collect and collate all of the knowledge available to us within the Sanatani tradition.

In the context of IKS, the term Systems refers to structured frameworks of thought, practices, and disciplines developed in ancient and classical India that span various fields of knowledge. These systems are holistic and interdisciplinary, addressing subjects such as philosophy, science, arts, medicine, and governance. The key components are Philosophical Systems (Darshanas etc), Medical Systems (Ayurveda, Siddha), Linguistic and Grammatical Systems (Pānini), Mathematical Systems, (Aryabhata, Varāhamihira. Brahmagupta, Bhāskara), Artistic and Aesthetic Systems: Political and Economic Systems (Arthshāstra, Nitisastra), Environmental and Ethical Systems, Spiritual and Ritualistic Systems. Systems refer to the manner in which these items are integrated into a holistic unity that is both contextual and practical.

In summary, IKS is intimately connected with our ancient scriptures. The Nyāya Darshana, or school of thought, centres on logic and epistemology, emphasizing rational inquiry to attain knowledge and truth. Key features include methods of debate, valid sources of knowledge (perception, inference, comparison, and testimony), and techniques to distinguish valid reasoning from fallacies. Its foundation is in Indian philosophy for developing rigorous logical methods. IKS is similarly based on a methodology of rigorous questioning and rejection of fallacies that fail the tests of logic. In the context of the scientific disciplines, the Vaiseshika Darshana focuses on categorizing reality into fundamental elements or dravyas. It emphasizes atomism, proposing that all physical substances are composed of indivisible atoms. Key features include exploring six categories or padārthas: substance, quality, action, generality, particularity, and inherence, aiming for liberation or moksha through knowledge of these universal principles. The strong influence of holism is again shared with IKS which should be imparted with the goal of being able to solve advanced scientific problems of the modern age.

There is little doubt that the time is ripe for an educational revolution in India. For too long, we have struggled with a system that had its roots in the Macaulay dictum and was then further corrupted after independence by a situation where a very limited amount of funding was available to educate a population that was just around 12-18% literate. This number has risen to 77% today but let us remember that being technically literate does not mean that one is educated. We still limp along and there is little connection between formal education as expressed by a school or college degree and employability. The economic problem more or less spontaneously led to a social problem with the limited funding available for education being cornered by special interest groups with political influence—an educational jati system. This was formalized in the institutionalization of reservations, initially for the SC ST communities but later going up to a minimum of 49.5% across the country with the inclusion of the OBC group, and further delinking merit from outcomes (in Tamil Nadu this number is an absurd 69%). Realizing these almost insurmountable contradictions between aspirations and abilities, the governments of the day sporadically instituted various commissions to look into the education system and make recommendations, specifically in 1948, 1964, 1986, and most recently in 2020, the National Educational Policy (NEP 2020). Most of the recommendations of these committees never saw the light of day.

It is in this disappointing context that one must look at the Indic Knowledge System (IKS) initiative, which attempts in its own way, a reversal of the education pattern to a system that is more reminiscent of what prevailed in this country before Macaulay, in other words, to go back to a cognitive system that relied on holism, inductive logic, and intuitive thinking. Holism is the essence of IKS and it embodies the holistic and integrative wisdom of ancient India, covering diverse domains like science, art, medicine, philosophy, and spirituality. Unlike modern Indian education, which often focuses on rote memorization and standardized testing, IKS nurtures critical thinking, contextual knowledge, and values-based education.

Rooted in texts like the Vedas and Upanishads, IKS emphasizes experiential learning, ethics, interconnectedness, and lifelong inquiry. There is no doubt that IKS is derived from Sanātana Dharma, and no one should artificially try to conflate it with woke ideas of Nehruvian secularism or try to integrate it with concepts that are unique to the Abrahamic faiths. The twain do not intersect, and IKS is and will only be a part of the Hindu Rashtra that is eagerly awaited by an overwhelmingly large section of our population, namely the 80% Hindus of India. IKS is based in the Hindu religion and as such it cannot be interpreted within the rubric of Abrahamic faiths.

India's NEP 2020 recommends integrating the IKS into the educational curriculum to promote a deeper understanding of the country's traditional wisdom, sciences, languages, and cultural heritage. This includes learning about ancient sciences, arts, linguistics, philosophy, and environmental conservation practices, along with modern subjects. The goal is to foster holistic education, instill pride in India's diverse heritage, and bridge the gap between traditional knowledge and contemporary learning methods.

Now, all this is very well but it simply restates what is known about the nature of IKS. How exactly do schools and colleges go about in this business and is it really possible to integrate IKS within a Macaulay system that is fundamentally different, in that the very cognitive processes in the two systems are diametrically opposite? One option is to not even try and mix these two streams but rather set up universities like Nalanda University or Rishihood University to operate wholly within the IKS pattern, more or less like Jewish Yeshivas that are based on Talmudic principles, and yet are able to turn out graduates that easily take their place in the secular world outside. Operationally, an IKS curriculum needs appropriate teachers and at present, we see the need for teachers with expertise in three different areas: (i) the domain expertise in the subject being taught; (ii) the Sanskrit language, and; (iii) a working knowledge of the Vedas. It will be difficult to find people with simultaneous expertise in all three areas till two or so generations of IKS students graduate at the PhD level. Faculty in IKS departments need therefore to be wisely chosen.

The Government of India needs to actively fund IKS programmes in private universities because many extraneous political factors might creep in if IKS is aggressively pushed in public universities especially state universities in Tamil Nadu and other places. IKS should be taken forward in as many places where there is eagerness and willingness to learn subjects through IKS. Once it is seen that there are employment opportunities for IKS-trained graduates, its popularity and relevance are bound to grow.

Overall, for IKS to be a practical reality in India, we need a civilizational reworking, in other words integrating India's re-awakening with respect to its identity. IKS cannot be treated as a purely educational exercise, nor even as a subpart of the overall educational policy of the country as most recently articulated in NEP 2020. IKS can only have viability and relevance when a nation-state, namely India, remakes itself as a civilizational state, namely Bhārat.

This is a major exercise that needs reforms in all aspects of governance: the judiciary, the executive, and the legislature. The reforms should be directed towards a redefinition of the country as a Hindu Rashtra. For, if Sanātana Dharma lives, Bhārat lives—if Sanātana Dharma dies, Bhārat dies. Education can and must be viewed as a part of a grand design in which a country comes out of a millennium of physical, mental, intellectual, and above all, civilizational servitude.

The colonial mindset that has persisted even after 75 years of independence from Britain has been a really serious problem in India partly because the upper echelons of decision makers, the highest-level politicians and bureaucrats, were largely Macaulayist in their thinking till the mid-1970s, conservatively speaking. The diplomatic and organizational aspects of governance were, inter alia, gravely impaired. The matter of the rediscovery of India and its remaking as Bhārat its origins in the very nature of Sanātana Dharma.

The civilizational revolution is an immediate and short-term priority. The several policy and governmental changes during the past decade can only increase the feelings of self-confidence and self-pride among vast sections of Indians. We are mostly concerned here with the effects of the civilizational and cultural revolution on bringing in a dharmic educational system, governance institutions, and overall social regulation that will give a long-term, resilient thrust to India's economic expansion. It is in this context that IKS should be considered, and its practitioners should ideally be aware that the synergy of IKS with the overall movement towards a Hindu Rashtra can certainly lead to a fundamental change in our educational policies for the better.

> *My final scribbling is about what we will look like five years from now, politically speaking. The reader will notice that I have been plumb wrong in my very first prediction in this article. The BJP did not increase its 2019 tally of 303. It did not even secure 272 seats, a simple majority, forget about the 400+ that Modi wanted.*

Political Crystal Ball—Bhārat in 2030

Swarajya, 5 February 2024

Summary: Predicting the future is difficult in politics.

Recent events remind me of Winston Churchill's quip about the Japanese on the eve of Pearl Harbour when he said that "however sincerely we try to put ourselves in another person's position, we cannot allow for processes of the human mind and imagination to which reason offers no key".

What will be the outcome of the forthcoming Lok Sabha polls? I will not waste my time with a foregone conclusion — the BJP will get its simple majority, and possibly cross its 2019 tally.

More interesting is what the political dispensation will look like in the Bhārat of 2030, rather than in the India of 2024?

My analysis starts from the standpoint that the Indian voter is smart—he considers various options, also realising that he might have little contact with the person elected for a full five years. People like to vote but do not like to waste their vote. They have realised that politicians need them badly at the time of polling. They cast their vote for the party that most nearly approximates to their idea of who they are — and to their core identities.

Our general elections may be roughly divided into three phases: from 1950 to 1984; from 1989 to 2009 and; from 2014 onwards. The country gave a single party a majority in the Lok Sabha in the first and third phases. It did not do so in most of the 1989 to 2014 interregnum. The 1991 result, like the 1984 one, was a freak result arising from a political assassination.

The first phase saw a force feeding of half-baked liberal, socialistic and so-called secular ideas down the throats of a largely poor, unthinking people who were still coming out of the trauma of the colonial era and partition. These ideas mutated in the second phase, with concepts of regionalism and linguistic chauvinism thrown in. A number of regional, dynastic, political parties came into existence and held their state satrapies in a firm grip.

By the 1990s, the Nehruvian idea of India was largely a fiction in the drawing rooms of Lutyens Delhi and the lounges of the India International Centre, the heart of the imaginary liberal empire. On the ground, however, in the states, it was regionalism, casteism and linguistic jabberwocky that ruled the roost.

The regional parties found great comfort in joining coalition governments at the Centre as it allowed each satrap to consolidate himself or herself in their satrapy, and increase their patronage, influence and of course their bank balances. The Centre became debilitated and weak. There was effectively no real idea of India from 1989 to 2014.

The rise of Bharatiya Janata Party (BJP), through the disputed structure demolition and the long years till last month's pran pratishtha, has paralleled a social and cultural reawakening among all Indians as the nation found itself finally as a Hindu Rashtra. The BJP defined and refined a national alternative to the false secularism of the Congress. It testifies to the acumen and patience of the Rashtriya Swayamsevak Sangh (RSS) and the BJP (including its previous avatars) that they were able to so correctly judge the nature of the Hindu in

Bharat and persist with their convictions for a full century before achieving their stated aim of Hindu Rashtra.

The spontaneous outpouring of emotion, which went far beyond political loyalties, has finally established that Hindus like being Hindus and for the first time they are not afraid to say so openly. At this inflection point, what are the possible political contours of the Bhārat of 2030?

The rise of national consciousness, must see the inevitable downfall of the regional parties and a concomitant decline of dynasty. As the country becomes richer, citizens will pay far less attention to language, caste and regionalism for example about things like why Odias and Banglas in Bengaluru are unable or unwilling to speak in Kannada. Malayalees will stop arguing about the greatness of a bankrupt Kerala. People will be more worried about jobs, their children's education, housing, clean water, and amenities such as rapid transport systems and security on the streets. An ageing population will want better healthcare and security. Very few will vote for a Kurmi just because he is a Kurmi or vote against a Brahmin just because he is a Brahmin, even in Tamil Nadu. Muslims might actually vote for the BJP. There will be an increase in inter-caste marriages. This is what a stronger economy means. Cultural awareness drives the economy and a stronger economy drives social progress.

There are around 200 Lok Sabha constituencies where the BJP has not won at all since 2004. In some of these cases, the BJP did not contest, as part of a seat-sharing arrangement with an ally (Maharashtra, Bihar, Punjab) but it does appear that there are still around 150 seats where a BJP victory is practically impossible in the near future. Politics abhors a vacuum and it is inevitable that with a decrease of regionalism, there will be a national coalescence of political forces in these areas that would appeal to the voter in ways the BJP does not or cannot. The way would accordingly be paved for a genuine two-party system, the ideal for a parliamentary democracy with first-past-the-post voting. Four possibilities will be enumerated for the consideration of the reader.

The first possibility is that of the appearance of a rejuvenated Congress that has discarded the baggage of its first family in all ways including the physical disappearance of all blood descendants of Jawaharlal Nehru from the country. This is not as far-fetched as it might appear. Political revolutions in other countries are often accompanied by the removal or expulsion of unpopular leaders and the continued incompetence of the family in being unable to secure electoral victories for the Congress might be enough for an internal bloodbath. A Congress without the family might attract a respectable number of middle of the road citizens whose fondness for Nehruvian secularism is still so strong that they can never bring themselves to vote for the BJP. Without the family, I suspect that the Congress can easily assume the second political place in a majority of the states.

The second possibility considers the intransigence of the first family to vacate their pole position, leading to the demise of the Congress. In this situation, a new national alternative could emerge from those who share the concepts of appeasement secularism and soft socialism but are more politically savvy than the Congress. Such a national party might not have a distinctive ideology of its own, but this in itself would appeal to Hindu voters who abhor the BJP as being anti-Muslim or have strong feelings of self-loathing brought about by stubborn Macaulayism. These are the Hindus who call themselves spiritual but not religious and feel that Hinduism is not a religion but a way of life. They say they are apolitical but want a strong opposition. These form the bulk of the 20 per cent committed Congress voters in the country today and urban non-voters. They might have hoped that the Aam Aadmi Party (AAP) was going to be a credible alternative to the Congress but the shenanigans and corruption in the AAP has put paid to this. There is a chance that this rainbow coalition of religious minorities, affluent upper castes, victims of reservations and non-practising Hindus can command a tenacious block of 25 per cent or so of the national vote against the BJP.

Such a bloc could never beat the BJP in the Centre in a first-past-the-post system but they would form a solid opposition that could attack the BJP inside and outside Parliament on issues rather than on personalities.

The third possibility considers that a left liberal alternative forms within the BJP itself. This might happen in the event of the second possibility being a non-starter. A new grouping may not find enough traction to forge a national consensus a bit like INDI Alliance today.

As the family might not yield control of the Congress, the regional satraps might not yield control of their individual outfits. In such a case, and since politics abhors a vacuum, a left alternative might well carve itself out from the BJP. The BJP is becoming very large today as the Congress had become by 1970, accommodating several economic ideologies within it.

The Congress gradually split but the breakaway units kept to their regions rather than staying national. In the BJP, cultural ideology is strong, and so the fragmentation might not become dissipative. We might see a leftist, liberal, but still nationalistic, version of the party along with a more rightist, conservative version, with both parties placed well within the ideological ambit of the parent organisation, namely the RSS. Hindu Rashtra would then be complete and with it any memory of Jawaharlal Nehru would have been erased completely from our consciousness.

The final possibility considers that future political developments in India are directed by world events of a gigantic nature. The first possibilities have only discussed happenings and personalities within India. If, on the other hand, the US, Europe, China and West Asia move towards a Third World War like situation, it would be impossible for Bhārat not to be drawn into such a conflict. Each of the previous world wars led to a reconfiguration of empires, countries and nations. The Third World War would be no different. The great ideals that this country has always stood for, duty, tolerance and understanding, might well gain centre stage in a new world order and Bhārat as an exponent of the Vasudhaiva Kutumbakam philosophy might not be such a far-fetched fancy. This situation might become inevitable for the world for economic rather than political reasons. In this case, all bets on how 2030 would look are off, and it would be anyone's guess. Borders would be redrawn, Pakistan might disappear and a non-political entity called Bhāratavarsha might become the sphere of influence for the political entity we call Bhārat.

The present situation of a strong BJP and a splintered opposition, is not stable. At best it is metastable, and these conditions move rapidly to the nearest stable condition, the one that is obtained the quickest even if it is not the best. In chemistry, we call this kinetic and thermodynamic control. If politicians study this subject, they would realise that kinetics usually wins unless the temperature is very high.

Which of my four possibilities can we get to the fastest? Or will we achieve the best?

> *I don't see a fifth possibility. Some readers might foresee a split of India itself, perhaps a north south divide? This cannot happen unless India is weakened considerably vis-à-vis the USA and China—and this seems unlikely at least in 2025—and not with*

Trump behaving as he is behaving today, driving India into China's arms with his tariffs.

And finally, I want to draw the attention of the reader to my analysis of India in terms of what its fate has been in the context of cyclical time rather than in terms of linear time and chaotic time, taking from the ideas of William Strauss and Neil Howe. If one goes with the cyclical time model, four turnings of around 20 to 25 years each form a saeculum in world history and India seems to have entered its fourth turning around 2010, a period where we may see much unrest and collapse before we enter a new 80-100 year cycle around 2035.

Epilogue

India at the Fourth Turning

Sunday Guardian, 3 August 2025

The present time is one of the most intriguing and unusual for any moderately intelligent Bhāratiya observer, born and living in this country. The past is being forgotten rapidly, the present, while puzzling, is full of promise, and the future, as is usually the case, is substantially unpredictable. If one reckons that our civilization is 5000 years old, it ran a normal course for ~4000 of these before a cataclysmic encounter with alien forces and influences debilitated it to such an extent that by the end of the last 1200 years (Muhammad bin Qasim invasion of Sindh in 712 to the BJP Lok Sabha victory in 2014) its very existence as a civilization had come under serious threat. Unexpectedly, the last decade has seen a fundamental shift in the way many Bhāratiyas, living in their country, perceive it. This perception is not political, although it is easy enough to dismiss it as such. I would say it is rather a matter of feeling a unifying identity as a Bhāratiya, an inhabitant of an ancient land coming to terms with living an honourable life in a new country.

Bhārat in 2026 is part of a world that was organised in a very specific and tight way during the past eight decades following the end of World War II, and which organization is now rapidly unraveling. This organization was largely economic, and used technological prowess and military power to enforce an American rules-based order that secured the economic interests of the powerful Western world, essentially the G7 countries and their auxiliaries. The Soviet bloc played some role in limiting the total hegemony of the West but their experiment did not last long and by 1990, one was talking about a monopolar American world. If nothing had changed, India, as I would like to call it then, would have eventually succumbed to its natural disadvantages, and become a client of the West in one way or another.

It was at this stage (late 1990s) that the remarkable rise of China, facilitated ironically by America, brought in new economic equations into the global geopolitical scenario and the world, once again, was assuming bipolar character. Simultaneously, and possibly because of the rise of China, India came below the radar level of the West, and in its inimitable way began a slow and painful climb up the economic ladder helpfully ignored by the West. The better economic position of Bhārat today is largely due to its demographic dividend paying off to some limited extent, and also to the fact that the chances of any Congress dominated dispensation at the central government level are now very slim.

Bhārat is not a rich country in 2026 but it is not poor either. China and America will try their best to slow down its economic growth and it will need all our geostrategic skills to thwart these two superpowers at least till we touch the $7-8 trillion level, for after that, our rapid rise cannot be stopped. In the interim, it is the duty of any central government to strike a balance between rapid economic growth and the rise of income disparities. No country has come up economically avoiding income disparities totally.

Bhārat simply cannot rise economically if the outmoded doctrine of socialism is given a free run. On the other hand, and in a positive sense, every increase in our GDP will reduce the likelihood of fissiparous tendencies like caste, language and religion taking the front seat in our socio-economic discourse making these negative factors rapidly irrelevant.

Combining economic and civilizational factors, it is fair in my view to suggest that it is the present awakening of Sanātani consciousness that will provide the unique Bhāratiya fillip that will precede a non linear upward rise of our economy. Each country that became powerful did so by using a peculiar advantage that it alone possessed. This was manufacturing and commerce for America, colonial-based mercantilism in Britain, militarism in Germany and possibly cultural outreach in France. Bhārat will need to leverage its civilizational heft as it enters higher reaches of S&T that alone can guarantee entrance into the higher world of economic and military power.

The gradual though not complete decline of America and China and the hopefully concomitant rise of Bhārat will see more parity in international relationships during the next decade. By 2035 I foresee a world that will become the playground of four empires, America, China, Bhārat and Russia, rather than a patchwork of nation-states, organic or artificial. The concept of the nation-state, itself an idea that was exclusively European, has become less important with the dwindling of Europe as a dominant influence in world affairs. Europe faces hard choices and needs to position itself between the Amerisphere and the Eurasian sphere. Mackinder's geographical pivot of history is being remade but rather than being Eurocentric it is now geocentric.

The exact course of events will be determined by the nature of the leaders that are thrown up in different parts of the world, and completely unpredictable events, unpredictable not in the events themselves but in terms of their long term consequences. Mehmet II's capture of Constantinople in 1650, the forced abdication of King James II in England in 1688, Gavrilo Princip's assassination of Archduke Ferdinand in Sarajevo in 1914 and the attack on Pearl Harbor by the Japanese military in 1941 come to mind. It is in the prediction of such events that the acumen of skilled observers will be put to test. As the famous Hungarian-American nuclear physicist Leo Szilard put it, and as I have said in the Prologue of this book, it is not necessary to be more intelligent than others, but just one day quicker in expressing your thoughts. And this need not be difficult if one realises that we live in a world of four turnings, one that is characterized by a cyclical time of High, Awakening, Unraveling and Crisis, rather than in a linear time of gradual all round improvement, and further that we are just entering the fourth turning of the 80 year saeculum now.

It is this spirit that has prompted much of my thinking and scribbling over the past three decades, some examples of which have been presented in this book.

Index

M

N

O

P

Q

R

S

U

V

Z

URBAN NAXALS: The Making of Buddha In A Traffic Jam

Vivek Agnihotri

978-1942426059 I ₹ 499 I PB

Urban Naxals reveals Vivek Agnihotri's journey to expose the urban network behind India's Maoist insurgency—leftist academia, media, NGOs—through his film's struggle, screenings, and the ideological war that followed.

LOVE JIHAD OR PREDATORY DAWAH?

Monika Arora, Sonali Chitalkar, Shruti Mishra, Monicca Agarwaal

978-1942426639 I ₹ 299 I PB

This book explores interfaith relationships involving Muslims and non-Muslims, revealing real-life stories, legal issues, Sharia conflicts, and ideological motives—questioning whether such alliances are rooted in love, dominance, or religious conversion.

ALL RELIGIONS ARE NOT THE SAME

Sanjay Dixit

979-8885751414 I ₹ 399 I PB

Sanjay Dixit systematically explains key distinctions among world religions, highlighting Sanatana Dharma's completeness as a universal system. Free from political correctness, the book offers clarity, depth, and rational spiritual insight.

MODI AND ME: A Political, Cultural & Religious Reawakening

Saurav Dutt

979-8885751407 I ₹ 399 I PB

This incisive book explores Hindu nationalism's rise under Narendra Modi, its role in countering Hinduphobia, and its impact on India's politics, society, and global standing amid ideological and cultural conflicts.

UNBREAKING INDIA: Decision on Article 370 and the CAA

Sanjay Dixit

HB 978-1942426431 I ₹ 799

PB 978-1942426356 I ₹ 499

This book offers a well-researched, lucid analysis of Article 370's removal and the enactment of CAA, tracing their historical, legal, and political roots, and examining their contemporary relevance and constitutional significance.

THE MAJORITARIAN MYTH: How Unscientific Social Theories Create Disharmony

Kausik Gangopadhyay

979-8885751582 I ₹ 449 I PB

This thought-provoking book challenges the flawed idea of majoritarianism using logic, science, and philosophy—revealing how intolerance arises not from numbers, but from ideologies like the Linear Theory of Social Evolution.

About the Author

Gautam Desiraju has been in the Solid State and Structural Chemistry Unit of the Indian Institute of Science, Bangalore, India since 2009, and since 2023, he has been a Distinguished Visiting Professor in UPES, Dehradun. Prior to this, he was in the University of Hyderabad for 30 years. He has played a major role in the development and growth of the subject of crystal engineering. He is noted for his role in the concept of weak hydrogen bonding gaining acceptance among chemists and crystallographers. His books on crystal engineering (Elsevier, 1989; World Scientific, 2011) and the weak hydrogen bond in structural chemistry and biology (OUP, 1999) are particularly well known. He is one of the most highly cited Indian scientists with more than 475 research papers, 80000+ citations and an h-index of 105. He has won international awards such as the Alexander von Humboldt Forschungspreis, the TWAS award in Chemistry, and the ISA medal for Science of the University of Bologna. He has guided the Ph.D work of around 35 students and mentored around 70 post-doctoral associates. He is a member of the editorial advisory boards of *Chemical Communications* and the *Journal of the American Chemical Society*. He is a former president of the International Union of Crystallography. He is a recipient of an honorary doctorate degree of the Universidad Nacional de Córdoba, Argentina, Rayalaseema University, Kurnool and Gulbarga University, Kalaburagi. He was awarded the Acharya P. C. Ray Medal (2015) of the University of Calcutta for innovation in science and technology.

His books *Bhārat: India 2.0* and *Delimitation and States Reorganization* are outside the scientific domain and are concerned with the constitutional history of India and its re-imagination as Bhārat, a civilisational state rather than a nation-state as has been understood till now. Two books published in 2025 are *India's Supply Chains in a World at War* and *Fixing Science in India: A Socio-Economic Prescription*. A scientific autobiography for the Gesellschaft Deutscher Chemiker (German Chemical Society) in their series *Lebenswerke in der Chimie (Lives in Chemistry)* will appear in 2026.